NEWLY COMMISSIONED NAVAL OFFICER'S GUIDE

NEWLY COMMISSIONED NAVAL OFFICER'S GUIDE

CDR FRED W. KACHER, USN

NAVAL INSTITUTE PRESS
Annapolis, Maryland

Naval Institute Press
291 Wood Road
Annapolis, MD 21402

Library of Congress Cataloging-in-Publication Data
Kacher, Fred W.
  Newly commissioned naval officer's guide / Fred W. Kacher.
    p. cm.
  Includes bibliographical references and index.
  ISBN 978-1-59114-426-7 (alk. paper)
  1. United States. Navy—Officers' handbooks. 2. United States. Navy—Military life—
Handbooks, manuals, etc. I. Title.
  V133.K33 2009
  359.00973—dc22
                                        2009025840

Printed in the United States of America on acid-free paper

19 18 17 16   7 6 5 4 3

Book layout and composition: David Alcorn, Alcorn Publication Design

Contents

Acronyms

3M	maintenance, material, and management system
AMC	Air Mobility Command
API	aviation preflight indoctrination
ARI	alcohol related incident
ASW	antisubmarine warfare
ATRC	Aegis Training and Readiness Center
BAH	basic allowance for housing
BAS	basic allowance for subsistence
BOL	BUPERS On-Line
BUDS	basic underwater demolition
BUPERS	Bureau of Naval Personnel
CAC	common access card
CAS	collaboration at sea
CBQ	combined bachelor's quarters
CDO	command duty officer
CEC	Civil Engineer Corps
CECOS	Civil Engineer Corps Officer School
CFC	Combined Federal Campaign
CFL	command fitness leader
CFS	command financial specialist
CIA	controlled industrial area
CIC	combat information center
CICWO	combat information center watch officer
CMC	command master chief
CMEO	command managed equal opportunity
CNO	Chief of Naval Operations
CNT	certified navy twill
CO	commanding officer
COMREL	community relations
CPO	chief petty officer
CWO	chief warrant officer
DAPA	drug and alcohol prevention advisor
DFAS	Defense Finance Accounting Service

DIMS	daily intention messages
DINFOS	Defense Information School
DITS	Division in the Spotlight
DoD	Department of Defense
DOSP	division officer sequencing plan
ED	engineering duty
EDA	expected date of arrival
EDD	expected detachment date
EDO	engineering duty officer
EOOW	engineering officer of the watch
FAO	foreign area officer
FAP	Family Advocacy Program
FFSC	Fleet and Family Support Center
FISC	Fleet Industrial Supply Center
FSA	family separation allowance
FTS	full-time support officer
HR	human resource officer
IO	intelligence officer
IP	information professional officer
IW	information warfare officer
JAG	judge advocate generals
JCCS	Joint Crew Composite Squadron
JFTR	Joint Federal Travel Regulations
JO	junior officer
JPME	joint professional military education
LCPO	leading chief petty officer
LDO	limited duty officer
LES	leave and earnings statement
LPO	leading petty officer
MCPON	Master Chief Petty Officer of the Navy
MSFD	main space fire doctrine
MWR	morale, welfare, and recreation
NATOPS	naval air training and operating procedures standards
NAVSUP	Naval Supply Systems Command
NJP	nonjudicial punishment
NPRP	Navy Professional Reading Program
NROTC	Naval Reserve Officers Training Corps
OCE	officer conducting the exercise
OCS	Officer Candidate School
ODC	officer data card

OMPF	official military personnel file
OOD	officer of the deck
OSR	officer service record
OTC	officer in tactical command
PAO	public affairs officer
PCS	permanent change of station
PFA	physical fitness assessment
PLR	PSD liaison representative
POA&M	plan of action and milestones
POD	plan of the day`
PQS	personnel qualification standards
PRD	planned rotation date
PSD	personnel support detachment
PSR	performance summary record
PT	physical training
SAVI	sexual assault victim intervention
SEAL	sea-air-land
SGLI	Service Group Life Insurance
SHIPSUP	shipbuilding superintendent
SNA	student naval aviators
SOBC	Submarine Officer Basic Course
SWO	surface warfare officers
SWSCO	surface warfare supply corps officer
TA	tuition assistance
TAD	temporary additional duty
TAO	tactical action officer
TDY	temporary duty
TPU	Transient Personnel Unit
TSP	Thrift Savings Plan
UCMJ	Uniform Code of Military Justice
URL	unrestricted line officers
VBSS	Visit Board Search and Seizure
WCS	workcenter supervisor
XO	executive officer
XOI	Executive Officer Inquiry

Preface

J ust like most endeavors related to the U.S. Navy, this book is the product of a multitude of naval leaders working together. Over the years, the *Newly Commissioned Officer's Guide* has taken several forms but all have conveyed the deep desire to help incoming generations of young naval officers entering the fleet. This edition owes a deep debt to the authors who wrote those previous editions.

As this new generation of ensigns "hits the fleet," they report to a Navy that is rising to challenges both traditional and transformational. Since this book's last inception, the emergence of information technology, the broader integration of women into the Navy, the attacks on September 11, and the ensuing global war on terror have all demonstrated that the naval service is an evolving profession. At the same time, many of the Navy's attributes and challenges remain as eternal as the sea, and ensigns of previous generations will still recognize many of the challenges that our new ensigns face today.

With this book, I have attempted to provide aspiring leaders with some of the benefits of a personal mentor. Because my experiences as a young ensign occurred some time ago, it was clear to me that the perspective of recent ensigns would be essential. I have been fortunate to benefit from the insight and talent of some extraordinary junior officers whose experiences as newly commissioned officers were much more recent than mine—this book would not have been possible without their help.

LT Jim Rushton served as the main driver of the book during the times when my professional duties precluded my giving this book the time it rightfully demanded. His efforts to pen five key chapters of this book have made his contributions truly irreplaceable, and I thank his wife, J'aime, as well for her editorial and emotional support. Sara Green, a superb division officer and shipmate, delivered a terrific chapter on basic divisional management. LCDR T. J. Zerr and LT John Liddle, two great division officers who served with me on USS *Princeton* and who continue to excel in the fleet as department heads, produced a first-rate chapter on naval policies. Finally, I thank LT Micah Murphy and LT Rob Niemeyer for their exceptional work in bringing the Navy's reading program alive for this book as well as compiling a useful Web site list that genuinely reflects what young ensigns rely on in the fleet.

I have also received superb editorial guidance from LCDR Chris Saufley, a wonderful friend and naval aviator, who volunteered to review the entire book to ensure that the experiences and lessons would benefit all ensigns instead of one specific service community. LCDR Brandon Bryan, a great surface warfare officer who will no doubt command again in the future, provided a sterling review of the entire draft as well. Mark Zeigler, a superb supply officer and writer, ensured that the line officer's perspective on pay and allowances remained "fair in the channel" with respect to the Navy's rules and regulations. I was also supported by my classmates in PCO Class 241—Ed Kaiser, Mike Lehman, Dave Glenister, Kristin Jacobsen, Mike Lockwood, John Zuhowski, Bryce Benson, David Wroe, Kathryn Devine—who improved the quality of this book with their corrections, comments, and advice. Any errors that remain after all the amazing help I have received from these writers and editors fall on my shoulders alone.

As I reflect on my own experience as an ensign, I would also like to thank CAPT Steve Lehr (Ret.), CAPT Rick Wright (Ret.), and CAPT Andy Pitts (Ret.), who loomed very large in my life as my commanding officers during my days as a division officer. I would also like to acknowledge CAPT Jake Ross (Ret.) and CAPT Joe Corsi (Ret.), who were both extraordinary mentors as I started to lead ensigns for the first time as a department head. Finally, I also thank CAPT Terry Culton, CAPT Chip Denman, and CAPT Jeff Wolstenholme, my commanding officers when I served as their executive officer—USS *Barry*'s record during your respective command tours looks even more impressive and admirable now that I am in command myself.

I am grateful to have worked for some senior leaders who were never too busy to share their insights and mentorship—ADM James Stavridis, VADM John Morgan, VADM Doug Crowder, VADM D. C. Curtis, VADM Pete Daly, RADM Phil Davidson, and CAPT Gerry Roncolato. Additionally, I thank Bryan McGrath, Vince McBeth, and Todd Leavitt, three extraordinary leaders just a few years senior to me who served as powerful role models and whose crews were honored to call them captain.

Just as leadership is essential in the fleet, it is also important in the production of a book. LCDR (Ret.) Tom Cutler has served as a superb coach, and his dedication to the naval service—both in uniform and in his current role as USNI's director of professional publishing—are without peer. Having been a complete novice in this process, I could not have asked for a better mentor or role model.

Lastly, I would like to thank my family for their support. My wife, Pam, has always been willing to read and reflect on my writing despite being an incredibly busy and dedicated wife and mother. I also thank my parents, Fred and Nancy Kacher, for serving as the original examples of leadership and patriotism in my life.

Leading as a new junior officer is both an art and a science. In some ways, ensigns are asked to do the improbable—lead with confidence and skill Sailors who are often older and more experienced than they are. Yet every generation of ensigns has managed not only to survive but to thrive in their roles as front-line leaders in the world's greatest navy. This book is dedicated to these young leaders—past, present, and future—who by their service make a difference in our Navy, our nation, and the world.

The journey begins. . . . (U.S. Navy, Shannon O'Connor)

Introduction

For newly commissioned officers opening this book, congratulations as you begin a new chapter in your life. As an officer in the U.S. Navy, you have embarked on a journey of consequence and purpose that will stay with you forever regardless of the path the rest of your life takes.

While no book can substitute for a great personal mentor, this book focuses on the very things a good mentor would pass on to you, one on one. As you read advice on "what to do and not do," be mindful that the path to success for a newly commissioned officer is not walked on a political tightrope in which you must avoid risk to survive and advance. Instead, take comfort that your leaders will expect you to learn and grow, and no ensign in history has completely avoided making a mistake. Far more important than avoiding mistakes is the importance of taking action—most naval leaders would prefer to have someone working for them who does ninety-five things out of one hundred correctly rather than someone who only does ten things perfectly in the same period of time. Planning, study, and practice will help you minimize mistakes (and hopefully not repeat old ones), but your leaders expect you to listen, lead, learn, and take action.

As you begin this life of action and leadership, you will quickly find that there are very few "silver bullet" solutions in life or in the Navy. Hard work, respect for your people, and staying positive are just a few of the traits that will always be prized in the Navy and other organizations that can also be described as "high demand, high reward" environments. Cramming for the test the night before rarely succeeds in life or in the Navy. As in sports, achieving success in the U.S. Navy will be the product of preparation, repetition, and effort that occur long before game day. You will see this principle reflected throughout this book—tomorrow's success depends on your hard work and preparation today.

Leaders at your commissioning source likely emphasized that accountability is the bedrock of our profession; your early experiences in the Navy will drive this point home vividly. Perception, smooth talk, and even subject matter expertise will not compensate for a failure to achieve results. You will find that this spirit of "results not excuses" permeates our service and is the watchword of the Sailors who will work for you. Because of this, the Navy is as close to a true meritocracy as we have in our society. No organization is perfect, but excellence and hard work are very difficult to deny in the U.S. Navy.

There is an old adage that says "the most important job you'll ever have is the one you have today." This is great advice no matter where you serve. Regardless of your long-term goal—or the desirability of your new assignment—if you focus your effort and talents on the job at hand, future opportunities will often fall into place. There is nothing wrong with planning for your future and aiming for long-term goals, but first you must be committed to give your very best to your current job.

Many former junior officers—whether they are admirals, chief executive officers, or among the seven presidents who have served as naval officers—look back at their early years of commissioned service as some of the most satisfying of their lives. Of course, few things worth doing come without hard work, and the life of a junior officer is one of both great opportunity and challenge. The goal of this book is to provide you the insights and tips for success that will help you make this journey a successful one. Welcome aboard!

★ 1 ★

LEADERSHIP
The Core of What We Do

Regardless of whether you have been commissioned with plans to serve as a SEAL or serve in the Supply Corps, as an officer in the U.S. Navy you will be expected to be a leader. As you begin training pipelines that are designed to equip you with the expertise and skills to perform your first duty assignment, you should never lose sight of this fact. Soon many of you will be placed in charge of Sailors who will be expecting you to provide them their course for the day and direction for their organization.

For those who have aspired to lead in the U.S. Navy, this first opportunity can be both exhilarating and a bit intimidating, but both feelings are understandable. As when you prepare before a big game or performance, it would be surprising not to feel a few butterflies before starting your first job. The good news is that you can take comfort that your training and the qualities that earned you a commission will help you to follow in the footsteps of the generations of ensigns who have gone before you.

While leaders can come in many shapes, sizes, and styles, following a few general principles will equip you well for your first year as an officer in the Navy. Whether you are in a training pipeline for quite some time after your commission or you expect to lead Sailors fairly soon after commissioning, these guidelines on leadership and personal behavior will help you succeed in the fleet.

Lead by Example

At first it may seem surprising that a new ensign will actually be expected to lead or provide an example for your more experienced troops, but that is exactly the case. In the very early stages at your first command, leading by example will largely focus on doing correct things on an individual scale, such as staying fit, wearing a good uniform, and carrying yourself in a positive but business-like manner. However, your ability to lead by example

1

will soon expand to include a focus on operational proficiency, efficient correspondence, and a demonstrated commitment to both your command and your Sailors.

Be Early

From our very first days of school, we have been taught to be punctual, so this advice may seem obvious. The demand for you to be on time becomes much more profound when your Sailors and your chain of command are also depending on your timeliness. Just as important, your commitment to be on time signals to those who lead you and to those you will lead that you respect their time and that they should respect yours. For many of you, real-world operational requirements will depend upon you and your subordinates being ready and on time to perform your mission.

Be Yourself

Demonstrate the positive qualities that ensured your success prior to entering the Navy. Being yourself does not imply that you "let it all hang out" by advertising your weaknesses. Instead, aspire to be your "best self," in a natural and authentic manner, by working modestly on your weaknesses and playing to your strengths. Do not pretend to be something you are not. If you are naturally a bit reserved or measured, do not try to be the loud cheerleader—you will not look comfortable, and Sailors will know when you are faking it. Instead, allow yourself to grow into your role.

Command Your Organization

Whether you are leading a traditional division on a submarine or ship or managing in an office environment, your leaders and your Sailors are going to expect you to take charge. Your Sailors will want to see you making decisions, leading evolutions, and showing interest in them and their work. Some new ensigns will very quickly take to their leadership role, but you may find it a bit uncomfortable to step into this role without having gained comprehensive knowledge in your field. Although you will want to do everything you can to prepare to lead in your respective service community, you will find that, as in life, you will rarely have perfect information to make a decision or take the lead on a project. Leading in the Navy involves managing risk, dealing with unknowns, and stepping up to your leadership role as soon as you can.

Focus on War Fighting and Operational Competence

The U.S. Navy is an operational fighting force, so the majority of newly commissioned officers will be assigned to an operational job, whether it is flying an aircraft, driving a ship, or participating in ground missions. In many cases, you will quickly be expected to lead your Sailors while conducting tactical operations or efforts that support combat operations. More broadly, your Sailors may look to you for guidance and information on greater naval roles, missions, and policies, so be ready to dedicate yourself to becoming an eternal student of the naval profession.

Set the Standard

Whether you are conducting a daily cleanliness assessment of your workspaces, evaluating written reports, or leading a debrief of a tactical evolution, you will have many opportunities to signal your standards to your Sailors. Although some Sailors will always exceed your expectations, most will perform to the standards you set. If you accept untidy spaces, poorly written reports, or hastily executed drills, this is what you will continue to see. If, conversely, you professionally highlight the things you and your team need to work on and provide the team the opportunity to practice and train, you will almost certainly be rewarded with improved performance. Never walk past a problem; this will signal that you tacitly approve of the issue you ignored. Even if you are in a hurry, take a moment to point out the problem to a responsible Sailor in the space or write down the issue so you can discuss this with your senior enlisted leaders at a more opportune time.

Be Prepared to Deliver the Hard News

Whether you are debriefing your boss or providing feedback to your Sailors, leaders must have the courage to deliver the unvarnished truth. Tact and optimism are wonderful attributes; nevertheless, there will inevitably come a time when you must tell your team that their results did not match expectations, or tell your commanding officer that something is not going well. In the current age we live in, giving negative feedback is not something in vogue, but being able to constructively criticize and correct weaknesses will be necessary to move your people and your organization forward. No one wants to work for a negative leader, but providing clear, honest feedback as early as possible will prevent tougher situations in the future.

Integrity

You will be expected to choose the hard right over the easy wrong every time. Your assurance that a job has been completed or a maintenance check is satisfactory must be ironclad, and lives will depend on your commitment to do the right thing. The sea is an inherently dangerous environment, and it is no place for someone who cannot be trusted to tell the truth regardless of the consequences—your word must be your bond.

Be Courageous

For some ensigns, particularly those in the special warfare and aviation community, courage in the face of physical risks will be required on an early and regular basis. For other communities, you may be assigned rewarding but hazardous duties, such as serving maritime interception teams or on the ground in Iraq or Afghanistan, that will also challenge you to show courage. Every ensign, however, should be committed to show courage as a leader, courage as a human being, and courage to do the right thing.

Focus on Your Sailors

Although you are a new ensign, one job that starts right away is your duty to lead and care for those Sailors under your leadership. The paradigm of leading the "whole person" may seem intrusive compared to most civilian occupations where concern for employees ends when they depart their workplace. Everything from your Sailors' pay to their professional development is part of your leadership portfolio. This does not mean that you will be able to approve every special request or leave chit that crosses your desk, but it is your job to support your Sailors so they can take care of the mission. Find a way to learn each Sailor's face, rank, and last name along with his or her family situation and goals.

While learning the details of your Sailors' lives may seem difficult, divisions at sea will have a division officer's notebook that captures this information. Even if you are not in an environment where a division officer's notebook is in place or practical, there are a number of ways to ensure that you have command of the details of your Sailors' lives. Some leaders have had their Sailors fill out index cards with relevant personal information that can be reviewed easily, and now many leaders use electronic versions on computers, BlackBerries, and personal digital assistants (PDAs).

Respect and Humility Go a Long Way

Although you may outrank your enlisted personnel, you will need to respect and rely on their expertise to succeed. Put another way, talent and knowledge are not always commensurate with rank. In certain areas of naval life, your junior Sailors who are working most closely with their equipment and performing day-to-day tasks may be the most likely people to provide solutions to some of the challenges your division or office faces.

Learn to Plan

Hope is not a strategy. As you progress as a leader, planning for broader operational challenges and for the future will become a key competency. While the uninitiated might think that planning and scheduling are for naval leaders more senior than a new ensign, you will be asked to plan and lead projects or operational evolutions in fairly short order. This opportunity to plan and oversee the execution of these efforts is one of the great opportunities that make our naval profession so special. Much like professional sports coaches who prepare their team for many more hours than the actual time it takes to play the game, you will often find that your efforts to plan an evolution will far exceed the time it takes to actually carry it out.

Remembering a few basics of naval planning will help you with this endeavor. First, recognize that you will find references and examples to guide you in your planning and execution for most of the challenges you will face. Second, you will often have department heads and senior enlisted folks who will help you in the planning process. Finally, remember that planning efforts almost always take longer than you think, so start the planning process early. Ultimately, by planning with attention to detail and with ample time, you and your team will have a sense of confidence as you begin to execute your plan.

Look Forward

Great leaders, even new ones, look beyond their in-boxes. Most of your Sailors will be focused on completing the immediate tasks before them, and rightfully so. As their leader, with the help of your department head and senior enlisted leadership partner, you will be expected to think beyond the day-to-day. Whether it is creating a plan to help your Sailors get selected for promotion or creating more opportunities to hone their tactical skills, you must always be looking ahead.

Listen to Your Senior Enlisted Leadership Partners

In most working situations that young ensigns encounter, your principal leadership partner will be a chief petty officer or leading petty officer. In your first few months at your new command, these senior enlisted leaders will be particularly valuable partners. As you gain experience, these relationships will evolve with you developing confidence and making broader decisions as time progresses. This progression is healthy and expected, but work hard to maintain positive relationships with your senior enlisted leadership. This does not mean that you should always defer to these leaders, and in rare cases you may have to deal with chiefs who are not performing well, but the poorly performing chief is by far the exception, not the rule.

Be a Good Follower

In addition to being a strong leader, it is just as important for you to be a good follower. As you lead, you will execute the visions and policies of your commanding officer and your department heads, and you will support broader naval policy in general. You will often be the person who articulates these policies and directives to your Sailors.

There may be times when you will not agree with the policies or plans you are being asked to support. There is a long-standing tradition of loyal dissent in the Navy, but this dissent must end when your leaders transition from deliberating a course of action to executing this decision. Your seniors will be counting on you to bring their policies to life with honor, courage, and commitment—the Navy's core values—just as you expect from your own subordinates regarding decisions you have made. Think of being a good follower in terms of the Golden Rule—follow your leaders as you want your subordinates to follow you.

HELPFUL HINTS: WHAT IS EXPECTED OF YOU—A QUICK TIP

Besides many of the obvious attributes that make a naval career so interesting and exciting, one of the benefits of working in a very mature organization is that there are usually well-articulated expectations and benchmarks to guide your performance. In this case, the fitness reports that your seniors will use to evaluate your performance include seven traits.

Professional expertise. Professional knowledge, proficiency, and qualifications.

Command or organizational climate/equal opportunity. Contributing to growth and development, human worth, community.

Military bearing/character. Appearance, conduct, physical fitness, adherence to Navy core values.

Teamwork. Contributions toward team-building and team results.

Mission accomplishment and initiative. Taking initiative, planning/prioritizing, achieving mission.

Leadership. Organizing, motivating, and developing others to accomplish goals.

Tactical Performance (warfare-qualified officers only). Basic and tactical employment of weapons systems.

While good fitness reports should be the by-product of great performance and not the driving force behind it, these seven attributes provide you a sense of what will be expected of you.

If the Navy Is New for You

For the prior enlisted officer who has just received a commission, the Navy's service and business culture will be familiar. For new ensigns starting their first full-time naval job after commissioning, it is worth touching on some basic tenets of naval culture that may not have been obvious from summer training and cruises. While some of these observations are not intrinsically related to the topic of leadership, understanding these cultural touchstones will help you lead more effectively:

You Are No Longer Living in a 9-to-5 World

In an unpredictable and dangerous world, it is not surprising that the Navy and the other armed services operate around the world twenty-four hours a day, seven days a week. The importance of your work and the excitement of real-world operations provide a vibrancy and variety that many career naval officers love. Operational considerations as varied as what time high tide occurs in a channel to the moonlight needed to complete a night ground mission may require that your work days begin very early or end very late relative to other professions—and those "workdays" will not always fall between Monday and Friday.

The Navy Starts Early

While the military's focus on getting an early start on the day is well known, a surprising number of new officers have struggled with the early starting times of the day—even in port. If you are on a ship, reveille usually occurs at 0600 on the weekdays, even if you are in port, and most shore commands begin their days between 0700 and 0800—still earlier than the average civilian workplace.

Timeliness Is a Core Virtue

While we discussed being punctual earlier in this chapter, it warrants additional mention for those who have not had much exposure to the Navy prior to earning their commission. Because so many more people will be counting on you to be where you need to be on time, you will find that timeliness has never been more important. It is very common in meetings around the Navy to observe those with experience arriving for a meeting five to ten minutes early and for those briefing to arrive much earlier than that. Simply put, making anyone—whether a seaman or an admiral—wait beyond a scheduled starting time of a meeting shows disrespect for his or her time.

You Are Part of a Watchstanding and Operational Culture

Whether you are working at a shore-based squadron (or office) that requires you to stand duty once a month or on a ship or submarine that requires you to stand watch several times a day, one of the Navy's universal skill sets is standing a good watch. No matter how quiet or mundane the duty, your

Leadership opportunities arise in many forms in a navy. Here two ensigns serve as boat officers in the Gulf. (U.S. Navy, MC2 Kitt Amaritnant)

leaders are counting on you to stand your watch or duty day professionally and with attention to detail. For young officers whose work and family experiences largely fall outside of the military, the notion of maintaining a presence in an otherwise empty building or command center outside of normal working hours may seem strange, but one of the first measures of your professional performance will likely be qualifying to stand a basic watch or duty position.

More profound than the watchstanding culture itself, you will either be directly involved in or be focused on supporting military operations. Even if your job is to track parts or file reports in support of an operation, it is important to remember what the broader mission is: delivering persistent combat power to fight and win—or prevent—our nation's wars.

Supporting Subordinates Is Defined Broadly

As a newly commissioned officer you will very likely be assigned a division officer role in providing "frontline" support for some of the Sailors under your command or at the very least in your workplace. While our greater society largely subscribes to the belief that only work-related conduct should be the concern of the employer when it comes to their employees' personal lives, the Navy takes a much broader view.

This broader view is not surprising given that the nature of our work demands that Sailors be ready to deploy on a moment's notice with protracted periods of absence from their families. Sailor's finances, educational needs, and family living arrangements—issues that would be left to employees to figure out on their own in civilian organizations—will often take up a surprising amount of your time. Like many things in life and in the Navy, an ounce of prevention often beats a pound of cure, so you will find that the very best leaders periodically check on their Sailors needs' rather than waiting for a crisis to occur.

You Will Be Running Things Faster Than You Think
In addition to serving their country, young officers most often cite early leadership opportunities as one of the most satisfying aspects of their jobs. In very short order, you will be running a watch team, leading a duty section, or overseeing an evolution at sea. Even if your first tasks are more administrative in nature, you will be expected to take the lead early, so be ready.

Read the Instructions
Whether you are preparing for a space inspection, conducting a flight deck emergency drill, or assisting in a burial at sea, you will find that there is a naval reference that will guide you in your preparation for the event and, where appropriate, its grading criteria. Even when challenges emerge that are not as specific as a training exercise, you will often find—with a little preparation and effort—that there are instructions, references, or lessons learned that can guide you in your preparation. One of the first questions you should ask yourself—and those who work for you—is "what is the reference?" because your seniors will surely be asking the same thing.

Leadership: A Universal Endeavor
Although each ensign will face a wide variety of experiences dictated by service community and individual circumstances, your role as a leader binds you together with your peers and the generations of officers who have gone before you. Your command, your Sailors, and, most importantly, your nation deserve nothing less than your very best.

Even in your first job, you will be making a difference. An ensign takes notes as he speaks with the master of a fishing boat during maritime security operations in the Persian Gulf. (U.S. Navy, MCC Daniel Sanford)

★ 2 ★

YOUR FIRST DUTY

Congratulations—you are a freshly commissioned officer in the U.S. Navy. College and your initial commissioning training are behind you, and you are ready to let the adventure begin. Like any new chapter in your life, you likely have more questions than answers. What happens now? What will be expected of you? How will you navigate the next few months as a newly commissioned officer—particularly if you are headed to an operational command right away? These are a few of the questions this chapter will help you answer.

You will find the next year to be challenging, to say the least. The period immediately ahead will be by turns exciting, interesting, sometimes difficult, and rewarding. You will discover more about your character and what you are capable of than many people will ever know in a lifetime. You are part of a long line of naval officers that stretch back to the dawn of the republic. Important work lies ahead!

Before You Report

The period of time before you actually check in to your new command will be a busy one. Packing, travel, and searching for a new place to live will absorb most of your time and attention. As you work through this period keep one thing in mind: Communicate. Keep your new command fully informed of your plans, whereabouts, and any personal issues that come up. Ask questions. Get as much done as possible in your personal life *before* you report. Life on a warship—or even a training command or office—is always busy (frequently bordering on hectic!), and your first few weeks will be especially demanding. There may be little time for things like searching for an apartment or unpacking, particularly if you are heading to an operational command.

As the day when you must actually report to your command approaches, you may feel a bit apprehensive. This is normal and it may help to remember that tens of thousands of young officers have been through the exact

11

same experience over the last two centuries; most have weathered the experience just fine. Within a few short weeks, you will be a fully acclimated member of your command.

Your Orders

As you neared commissioning, you will have received orders to your first command. You may or may not know exactly what job awaits you on your new ship or command, and you may or may not get some shore-based training en route. Your official Bureau of Naval Personnel (BUPERS) orders will tell you quite a bit, so take the time to read them carefully.

Part 1 of the standard official BUPERS order will be addressed to your current command, your new ship, and any intermediate training commands you will attend on the way to the ship. Note that after the "BUPERS ORDER" line it lists the sequential order number, your name, social security number, and your officer designator (in this case 1160 for a nonqualified surface warfare officer).

If there is a subsequent change issued to your orders (a not infrequent occurrence) a change number will appear after the BUPERS order number (i.e., "BUPERS Order: 0256 Change 1"). Note that under "Detaching Activity" and "Ultimate Activity" are two lines labeled EDD and EDA. These are your expected detachment date (EDD) from your current command and the expected date of arrival (EDA) at your new command. Finally, note the last line under "Ultimate Activity": Your "report no later than" date and time.

The First Page of Your Orders

Part 2 of your orders will provide a wealth of information in (relatively) plain language. Some of the things you will find here are specific directions to your detaching and ultimate commands to comply with various instructions such as security clearance requirements and medical screening. Further down assorted paragraphs will help you on your way, listing such things as contact points for government housing at your new duty station and advice on household goods shipment. If you have any additional questions, be sure to ask your leaders at your commissioning detachment before you depart. Part 2 will also give specific instructions to the detaching command on travel if your ship is homeported overseas or on deployment, which will be discussed in depth in the "Getting to Your Command" section below.

```
R 251042Z JAN 06
FM COMNAVPERSCOM MILLINGTON TN//PERS412/PERS455//
TO NROTC BIGSTATE
USS FASTSHIP (DDG 200)
BT
UNCLAS //N01321//
MSGID/GENADMIN/COMNAVPERSCOM//
SUBJ/BUPERS ORDER//
RMKS/
BUPERS ORDER: 0256    123-45-6789/1115  (PERS-4128)
OFFICIAL CHANGE DUTY ORDERS FOR
ENS CHESTER NIMITZ, USN
XXXXXXXXXXXXXXXXXXXXXXXXXXXXXXXXXXXXXXXXXXXXXXXXXXXXXXXXXXXXXXXXXXX
IN CARRYING OUT/PROCESSING THESE ORDERS, BOTH PARTS ONE AND TWO
MUST BE READ AND LISTED INSTRUCTIONS COMPLIED WITH.
XXXXXXXXXXXXXXXXXXXXXXXXXXXXXXXXXXXXXXXXXXXXXXXXXXXXXXXXXXXXXXXXXXX
PART  ONE
------- DETACHING ACTIVITY (M) -------
WHEN DIRECTED BY REPORTING SENIOR, DETACH IN SEP 06    EDD: SEP 06
FROM STU NROTC BIGSTATE                   UIC: 31405
PERMANENT DUTY STATION  CA, SAN DIEGO
FROM DUTY UNDER INSTRUCTION               ACC: 342
PERSONNEL ACCOUNTING SUPPORT: PERSONNEL SUPPDET NAVPOSGRADS
UIC: 43073
------- ULTIMATE ACTIVITY (M) -------
REPORT NOT LATER THAN OCT 06              EDA: OCT 06
TO USS FASTSHIP (DDG 200)                 UIC: 30465
PERMANENT DUTY STATION  VA, NORFOLK
FOR DUTY                                  ACC: 342
BSC: 99990
PRD: 0704
PERSONNEL ACCOUNTING SUPPORT: PERSUPPDET NORFOLK
UIC: 43099
- REPORT NOT LATER THAN 0700, 10 OCT 06.
------- ACCOUNTING DATA -------
MAC CIC: 3N3I65564177460
CIC: A83I62UM
PCS ACCOUNTING DATA:
N3I6 1761453.2251 T 068566 A8 3I6/2/U/M 3I6556417746
```

Your Sponsor

When your new command receives a copy of your orders they will assign a sponsor to assist you with your transition and guide you through your first few weeks. Within a week or so, you should get a package in the mail from your sponsor with an introductory letter, contact data, and information on your new command and homeport.

If you do not receive word within a few weeks, or if you simply cannot wait to get started, contact the ship to find out who your sponsor is. The best way to do this is to send an e-mail to your new XO or Department Head (you may have to make a creative guess at the e-mail address, but it will usually be similar to xo@ddg50.navy.mil or ops@cg47.navy.mil. Failing that, do an Internet search for the command's website and send an email to the webmaster, asking for the sponsor coordinator and your Department Head. One note: on smaller operational commands you can expect to see more tailored outreach to you as a newly arriving crew member; if you are heading to a shore command or training command, your contact with your new command may be a bit less personal.

Your sponsor's job is to answer questions, act as an intermediary between you and the ship's office (admin) on travel matters, and generally smooth your way. Not all sponsors are created equal—if you are not getting the information you need, then politely request the answers, but keep in mind that your sponsor is likely very busy in his or her own right, running a vital part of a ship (or responsible for other substantial duties).

Writing a Letter to Your New Commanding Officer

"You never get a second chance to make a first impression" may be a cliché, but you should keep this in mind when you sit down to write a letter of introduction to your new commanding officer. It's not rocket science, but it does require some thought and attention to detail.

Your goal is to briefly introduce yourself, provide relevant contact information, fill the command in on any special personal issues that impact your immediate future, and give a sense of cheerful eagerness to get on with your new job. The letter will be read by your commanding officer (CO), executive officer (XO), and department head. Very likely, it will also make its way to your sponsor and the officer you will be relieving. Keep this in mind as you draft your letter; there are some rather infamous examples of poorly written letters of introduction floating around the fleet.

Below are a few tips on drafting your letter:

★   Be brief and to the point without being cold. It is okay to let some of your personality shine through, but don't bother with a lot of frivolous personal details.
★   Formal modes of address are appropriate. Find out the name of your new CO and begin with "Dear Captain XXX."
★   Don't try to be funny—humor rarely translates well on paper, particularly in your first communication with your new commanding officer.

★ Include a full list of contact methods (including addresses, phone numbers, and e-mail) and your travel plans between now and when you report aboard.

★ Give some brief personal details such as where you grew up, your commissioning source, and the name of your wife and kids (if applicable).

The above list is not intended to intimidate; it is presented merely so you can avoid some of the pitfalls that previous junior officers have occasionally fallen into. If you keep it positive and to the point and use the judgment that helped you earn your commission, your letter will serve you well.

Reporting to Your First Command

After receiving your orders and communicating with your new command, you will want to properly plan for the day you walk up to the quarterdeck of your new command. Recognizing that many new ensigns will be heading to training commands for their first assignment, reporting to an operational unit is often the most involved, so we will focus primarily on this challenge.

How Do I Get to My New Command?

When your orders are issued to an afloat command, your XO will work with the placement officer to send you to any schools that may be required for your specific job (termed "billet" in the Navy). In this case, the first leg of travel to intermediate schools is relatively straightforward. If you are traveling by commercial air, your sponsor will work with you and the ship's office to arrange an itinerary. Keep your sponsor informed! Before you leave, you will get an advanced travel payment to see you through until you check in, whereupon you will file a travel claim to be reimbursed for additional expenses.

If you have not received military decals for your car, you will very likely have to visit the pass and decal office on base (the guard at the gate will provide you guidance on what you need to do in this case). This process can take some time, so you may wish to do this a day or two prior to your reporting date. If your ship or submarine is at sea for a few days, you will usually check into the base Transient Personnel Unit (TPU) or into the squadron or strike group to which your command is attached. Once again, if you have questions as to where to report, reach out to your sponsor for advice.

This process is relatively simple if your ship is based in the United States and is not currently deployed. For commands or detachments based overseas, you will need to complete a thorough suitability screening process for both you and any family members you are taking with you to your

15

new homeport. Contact your new ship early and often—they will undoubt-edly be experts in this process if they are stationed overseas.

If your ship is deployed, you will need a "port call" message from the local transportation office. To arrange travel to the ship's port of call, you will want to know your ship's schedule. (Caution: A ship's movement information is usually classified data. You will likely not be able to talk about this openly on a commercial phone line or on the Internet.) Travel will be arranged one of two ways: If you are near a major naval base, your ship's office can probably arrange travel directly. If you are located at a Naval Reserve Officers Training Corps (NROTC) unit far from a naval base, you will likely report to the TPU in the ship's homeport before travel can be arranged.

Your First Day

Whereas many ensigns will report to a training command or office space ashore, those reporting to a ship or submarine will likely face a few more challenges. If this is the case with you, one of your first challenges will be to identify the pier where your ship or submarine is berthed, so be sure to e-mail or call ahead to your ship's sponsor to determine this information.

Once you have made your way to the ship's location, park near the command taking care not to park in a reserved space. You will need to pre-sent your ID to the Sailors guarding the gate at the end of the pier. Next to the pier, you will see your ship—a gray hull, bristling with antennas, guns, and activity. Above you, at the top of the brow (gangplank), you will see the officer of the deck (OOD) usually in dress uniform. Take a deep breath and get ready to begin your first day.

Checking Onboard

If you've haven't visited a naval ship recently, figuring out how to cross the brow properly can be a bit intimidating. You may want to pause for a few moments and watch somebody else cross the brow so you can get the lay-of-the-land. The sequence for reporting aboard is as follows:

★   Cross the brow to just before the gangway (the opening in the ship's rail). Face aft, come to attention, and salute the national ensign if you arrive on the ship between 0800 and sunset.
★   Face the OOD, salute, and say "Ensign Halsey, reporting as ordered."
★   Show the OOD your ID card (Tip: Get your ID card out of your wallet before you start up the brow) and step onto the quarterdeck.

The OOD will log your name in the deck log and call your sponsor. You should report aboard in summer whites (short sleeves) in the summer or dress blues in the winter. Bring your orders, medical record, and dental record.

What if your ship is in the shipyard? In this case, your ship may be deep in a controlled industrial area (CIA), covered with hoses and electrical cables. The best thing to do is arrange for your sponsor to meet you at the shipyard gate, with a hardhat and goggles. Failing that, report to the shipbuilding superintendent's (SHIPSUP) office and have them call the ship. Talk to your sponsor about what uniform to report in—while in the shipyard you may need to report in wash khakis and steel-toed boots.

If you are not reporting to an afloat unit or an intense training course such as basic underwater demolition (BUD/S, for sea-air-land [SEAL] training), your first day at a training command (or at an office) is likely to feel more similar to your previous training and academic experiences. If you are reporting to a shore command, you will want to read your orders, use the contact information included therein, and make an effort to ensure that your command knows the day you are coming. A member of the administrative team will likely endorse your orders, signaling that your leave or travel period is concluded, and you will start to follow a check-in process.

Almost all commands have a check-in process and a sponsor system, and your first few days will likely be dedicated to this endeavor. If you are first reporting to a training command, you can expect to be "in-processed" with your classmates en masse, so this check-in will likely resemble some of the precommissioning training check-ins you experienced previously. Regardless of what command you are reporting to, if it is possible, make a dry run the day before you report so you do not add to the stress of your first day by getting lost or failing to find a parking spot.

The Rest of Your First Day

The rest of your day will be devoted to introductions, administrative matters at the ship's office, and probably a quick tour of the ship. This may feel a bit disorienting, but you will soon get the hang of things. You may meet your CO, XO, and department head, but formal check-in interviews will probably be scheduled in the following days.

If you have reported to a ship or a command that is embarked on a ship, you will soon share a meal in the wardroom. We will discuss etiquette more fully in detail in a later chapter, but review the procedures for dining with your sponsor before lunch. If you are reporting to a squadron or a shore command, your lunch may be much more low-key with your command sponsor perhaps taking you to lunch on or near the base.

If reporting to a ship, you will also be assigned a bunk and locker on your first day. If you are fortunate, it will be a bunk in one of the officers' staterooms, but you may be assigned to a bunk in overflow berthing, a section of enlisted berthing that is used if there is an excess of officers assigned to the ship. While this arrangement is not as comfortable as a stateroom, remember that this is temporary as you will be shifted to a stateroom as more senior division officers rotate off the ship.

The First Few Weeks

Your first weeks at your new command will be a whirlwind of strange acronyms, turning over (taking responsibility for) your new division, and standing your first watches. Keep your eyes and ears open, and try to see as much as possible. The information below is presented to give you a sense of what to expect.

Indoctrination, Personnel Qualifications Standards, and Warfare Qualification

Your first week at a command will very likely be devoted to the administrative requirements of checking in and a formal introduction class often known as "Indoc." On a ship, this orientation session will teach you some basics like afloat safety and the ship's organization, and will touch on broader policy issues and regulations whether you are reporting afloat or ashore. One item you should ask for is the commanding officer's philosophy—it will likely be a one- or two-page memo that lays out the CO's vision and expectations.

Very soon after checking in at an afloat command, you will receive assignments related to the personnel qualification standards (PQS). PQS is the Navy's standardized system for qualification. It covers everything shipboard from how to conduct basic maintenance to the minimum knowledge standards required to qualify as the ship's tactical action officer (TAO). There will qualifications required for those serving ashore as well.

All PQS cards include a list of knowledge factors that must be mastered item by item. Most cards also include a variety of "practical factors" that involve actual physical demonstration of a skill by the trainee before it is "signed off." Watch station PQS, such as officer of the deck (OOD) and engineering officer of the watch (EOOW), will also require you to stand watches under instruction. The final step for most PQS will be a series of interviews, tests, and qualification boards (group interviews) designed to ensure readiness to assume your new responsibilities.

If you are reporting to a ship or submarine, one of your most important tasks over the next year or so will be earning your surface warfare or submarine warfare pin, which signifies your full entry into the ranks of the seagoing profession. Achieving this milestone will take a great deal of your time and energy during your first sea tour. Along the way to earning your pin, you will have to qualify for several watch positions, the most important of which is OOD.

Although you will have many other tasks and priorities vying for your attention, give the warfare qualification process the attention it deserves—there is nothing more important in your first tour than achieving surface warfare or submarine warfare qualification. In other communities, tactical competencies carry equal significance, although in some communities such as naval aviation and the special warfare communities you may have earned your warfare pin through an arduous training process prior to reporting to your first operational command.

Watchstanding

In many commands and on every ship, standing watch lies at the very heart of our profession. Your competence as a watchstander will be one of the primary skills by which your contribution to your command will be judged. Take this task seriously—you literally have the lives of your shipmates in your hands.

Very soon after your arrival you will be assigned a watchstation (on a surface ship you may be standing watch as conning officer on your first day under way). You should devote yourself to doing this job right, but take heart—your fellow officers will not let you fail. For a great deal of outstanding advice on watchstanding, see the *The Watch Officer's Guide* by ADM James Stavridis and CAPT Robert Girrier, available from the Naval Institute Press.

Your Division

Aside from qualification and watchstanding, the other great responsibility you will have is leading Sailors. On a ship or submarine, you will be directly responsible for a division of Sailors and, very often, millions of dollars' worth of equipment. If you are reporting to a shore billet you will likely be assigned some leadership responsibilities similar to the division officer's portfolio. Training, maintenance, administration, counseling, discipline, and ensuring the general welfare of your Sailors are just a few of the tasks that you will face.

Once again, take the job seriously, but do not allow yourself to become too anxious about how you will perform: your chief petty officer and more seasoned officers will spend a great deal of time teaching you the fundamentals of leadership and divisional management. For much more on the art and science of divisional leadership, see the superb *Division Officer's*

Guide, which opens with a quote from one of our greatest naval leaders, ADM Arleigh Burke, who remarked, "The division officer is the core of the Navy's spirit." Chapter 11 of this book discusses leadership and management for the newly commissioned officer in much greater detail.

Your Boss

In a typical afloat billet, your immediate superior will be one of the department heads (on most ships either the weapons officer/combat systems officer, operations officer, chief engineer, or supply officer). He or she will be responsible for up to one quarter of the ship's crew and equipment and many collateral duties, including the training of his junior officers and standing the most difficult watches on the ship. In other words, department heads will be very busy.

Regardless of where your first command is located, you will almost certainly be reporting to a department or branch head, a senior officer placed above you in a chain of command that leads to the commanding officer and the executive officer. As a division officer, you will work closely with your department head on the day-to-day operation of your command and planning for the future. A professional department head will do all he can to train and mentor you, but he will expect you to *lead* your division, look into the future, plan, carry out the policies of the commanding officer, and, most of all, *keep him informed.*

Basic Shipboard Organization

Not every ensign will be stationed on a ship; nevertheless, it is worth reviewing a ship's organization. You will see elements of this structure in most organizations you join as a newly commissioned officer. Most ensigns reporting to an afloat unit will serve as division officers, in charge of a group responsible for a specific set of equipment or tasks. Your division functions as part of a department with a broad portfolio of tasks vital to the ship's overall mission (i.e., engineering, combat systems, operations, supply). Your department head in turn reports to the executive officer, the second most senior officer on the ship who is directly responsible to the commanding officer for the overall operation of the ship.

The chain of command describes the interrelationships between the various levels of authority on a given ship, squadron, or shore command. This "chain" starts with the lowest ranking seaman or fireman, working up through work center supervisor, leading petty officer, leading chief petty officer, division officer, and department head, to the executive officer and commanding officer. The chain of command is in effect the nervous system of the command: direction flows down the chain while information flows up.

Each level in the chain of command is expected to execute the mission within its span of control and handle problems at the lowest level possible while keeping higher levels informed. This last element is especially important: "Keep the chain of command informed" is a mantra you will hear throughout your naval career (another popular saying is "Don't be the senior person with a secret"). You will often hear your leadership exhorting your Sailors to use the chain of command—and this is sound advice. Keep in mind that the ship's organization is not intended to be a "stovepipe" through which information is rigidly controlled—you will be expected to work closely with your peers in other divisions to solve problems and efficiently execute the command's mission.

If you are serving at sea on a surface ship, you will likely be initially assigned a watchstation such as a conning officer, reporting to the officer of the deck. This will quickly be followed by underway watch assignments leading to qualification as engineering officer of the watch (EOOW) and watches in the combat information center (CIC) such as combat information center watch officer (CICWO). Typically, you will stand one or two four- or five-hour watches in a day at sea, although this varies greatly with the pace of current operations and the number of persons qualified to fill out the watchbill.

In port, an ensign in an afloat assignment will often be assigned as in-port officer of the deck before moving on to standing one of the duty department head positions, responsible for a department in the absence of the department head (i.e., duty operations officer or engineering duty officer). You will report to the command duty officer (CDO), a seasoned officer responsible to the daily conduct of the ship's routine while in port.

You will also be assigned to a duty section soon after you check in. Duty sections have responsibility for the ship for a twenty-four-hour period while in port, during which you will likely be assigned one or two watches. The remainder of the day, you will be on board to supervise your department's duty section, act as a "damage control" reserve in the case of emergency, and defend the ship against outside attack. Most ships rotate through six or eight duty sections while in home port, and through three or four sections while deployed overseas.

If you are reporting to a training or shore command, your watchstanding and duty responsibilities may vary. Regardless of what watch or duty section you are assigned, you will want to approach the job seriously, work hard to get qualified so that you can return value to the organization, and, once qualified, aim to be ready to learn and fill the next senior position.

Some Basics on Shipboard Life and Naval Protocol

The U.S. Navy is an organization that prides itself on honoring tradition. Shipboard protocol is based on traditional military values and rituals that extend back to the birth of the U.S. Navy, and even further back to the Royal Navy. It exists as a common framework across the many generations of our Navy.

Like all military organizations, there exists a fine balance between deference to senior rank and the close bond between shipmates built up over months of close and difficult service together. That balance is always in play, and it is sometimes difficult for a new officer to discern the line between proper deference and the unique camaraderie of a military unit. This section is intended to help you navigate your first few months onboard. Below are some tips to orient you in the right direction.

Junior–Senior Officer Relationships

In theory, every officer onboard has a distinct seniority, based on rank and date of commissioning (a lineal number). In practice, most wardrooms or aviation squadrons are composed of three groups: the CO and XO, the department heads, and the division officers (often referred to as the "JOs," although technically any officer below the rank of commander is a junior officer). Relations between division officers will tend toward the informal use of first names (in private) while your relationship with department heads and above will be much more formal.

A nuance in this system is positional authority; sometimes an officer of junior rank is assigned to a job that entails supervision of officers technically senior, most commonly when a department head is junior to one of his division officers. In this case, precedence goes to whoever is senior by position, not rank (although sensible officers will certainly take actual rank into account when dealing with each other). When in doubt as to the lay of the land, tend to formality toward your seniors.

Relations with Enlisted Sailors

In the vast majority of naval communities, your default position here should be toward formality without being stuffy. Over time you will no doubt develop a certain amount of comfort with the folks who work for you. This is neither unexpected nor discouraged (after all, most of your Sailors are hard-working, smart, dedicated professionals, just like you). However, you must be careful to draw the line appropriately—occasional gentle joking or conversations about family are fine, but undue familiarity that tends toward a first-name basis must be discouraged. In all cases, you positively must avoid favoritism or fraternization, whether real or perceived.

Relations with Your Chief

How can you be expected to supervise a man or woman who is considerably older than you are and has much greater experience? This may be one of the thorniest issues you will encounter on your first tour. The quality of chief petty officers (CPO) can vary widely: at one end of the spectrum, you will be lucky enough to have a chief that can do her job (and yours) with ease; at the other—and much rarer—extreme, there will be CPOs who will need some prodding to fulfill their duties (to be fair, you will find the same phenomenon in the Officer Corps). Fortunately for the U.S. Navy, the vast majority of CPOs are highly competent and understand their role not only as divisional leaders but also as mentors of their division officers.

A sound approach to take toward your chief is an adaptation of President Reagan's saying, "Trust but verify." In other words, defer to your chief's skill and experience, but seek out the underlying facts for your own evaluation. "Chief, can you please show me the reference" is never a bad request, least of all for your own education.

Formality on Watch

There is no room for compromise regarding formality on watch. Sadly, this is a lesson that has been written in blood—informal communications have been the root cause of many a tragedy at sea. Formal repeat back of orders, focus on the task at hand, a questioning attitude, and strict adherence to established procedures are a must at all times when on watch.

After-Hours Protocol

Your entire wardroom will socialize together periodically, and you will almost certainly spend some time hanging out with your fellow junior officers. You will develop close friendships with your fellow JOs and to some extent with more senior officers. While a greater degree of informality will be expected in a social setting, the same basic shipboard rules on deference apply.

You will also on occasion interact with enlisted Sailors in a more social setting, at either command-sponsored functions or divisional parties. By all means, spend some time in conversation with your folks at the command picnic or make a brief appearance at a divisional party, but you must be careful not to cross the line into fraternization and undue familiarity. Think of it as a sort of "one drink" rule of thumb: spend enough time with your Sailors to converse over one beer or soda, then politely move on.

Common sense is a good guide to shipboard protocol and general etiquette, and both topics will be discussed in further detail later in this book.

Uniform Matters

The Uniform Regulations provide coverage of uniform matters in exhaustive detail. Every officer is expected to maintain a complete seabag of uniforms, and the importance of setting an example for your Sailors in terms of both having the right uniform and wearing it well cannot be overemphasized. This section gives a brief primer on uniforms for seagoing officers.

What Do Seagoing Officers Really Wear?

What you will wear under way will vary among commands. On ships and submarines, the two basic schemes are wash khakis and coveralls, each with steel-toed boots and a command ball cap. Most ships require wash khakis or coveralls on the bridge and fire-retardant coveralls in the engineering spaces. You will also be issued a foul-weather jacket for use on watch (this jacket is customarily not worn off ship).

When in port, you will routinely wear wash khakis, but you should always have a set of certified navy twill (CNT) "dress" khakis in hot standby on the ship—there will be many occasions when you will be required to greet a dignitary visiting the ship, visit a higher headquarters, or have a meeting off ship with little or no notice. If an aviator, you will most often wear a flight suit in your working environment but check with your more senior JOs to determine when a more formal uniform is required, for example, when visiting various parts of a base or dining in a more formal section of the wardroom on a ship. Finally, if you are a newly commissioned ensign serving at a shore command, you will likely be wearing CNT khakis, but uniforms will vary if you are attending an operational school.

What Else Should I Take with Me?

If you are reporting to your ship before deployment, you will have plenty of opportunity to figure out what to take under way with you. Be sure to confer with your ship's sponsor since he or she will have specific insight into what is normally worn and needed on the ship or command to which you are reporting. The basics include uniforms for in port and under way, the seasonal dress uniform, toiletries, physical training (PT) gear, professional reading, and clothes for liberty (bringing a jacket and tie or business attire for women is recommended).

Conclusion

As you prepare for one of the greatest transitions in your life, you will no doubt have many more questions than were answered here. Nevertheless, this chapter will get you headed in the right direction. Rest assured that within a few short weeks you will be a fully integrated member of your command, and within a year you will be a seasoned officer others will turn to for answers.

★ 3 ★

NAVAL CUSTOMS

Many organizations have their own unique set of customs, but very few organizations equal the U.S. Navy in the strength that our service draws from our traditions. As a newly commissioned ensign, you will likely encounter a greater variety of naval customs and courtesies than you did in previous chapters of your life. The good news is that the basics of naval courtesy and customs are not only relatively simple but have also been covered in commissioning pipelines such as the U.S. Naval Academy, Naval Reserve Officers Training Corps (NROTC), and officer indoctrination courses for those earning a commission from the fleet.

There are a number of books that do an exceptional job describing our service's customs. *Naval Courtesies, Customs, and Traditions* would be a fine addition to any naval officer's professional library; it covers both the current use and the history of the customs extensively. For a shorter but very practical overview of naval customs, refer to the *Bluejacket's Manual*, the definitive guide for Sailors of all ranks joining the naval service, which contains a superb chapter titled "Courtesies, Customs, and Traditions," which addresses the basics exceptionally well.

What Is so Special about These Customs?

If you have not spent much time in the Navy or as a member of a naval family, you may be wondering why these customs and conventions are so important and why those in the Navy spend so much time focusing on their appropriate observances and execution. Thomas J. Cutler, author of the centennial edition of the *Bluejacket's Manual*, explains it well: "Once you have been to sea, or flown on a naval air mission, or taken part in the many different things that Sailors the world over are doing every hour of every day, you will know from firsthand experience how different a job in the Navy can be from what your counterparts in civilian life are doing. It is only fitting, therefore, that we celebrate our uniqueness through special ceremonies and demonstrate our differences through special customs that remind us of our very different heritage."

To add to Cutler's superb explanation, these customs are in most cases fairly simple; they not only celebrate our heritage but also provide Sailors the opportunity to hone their attention to detail. As you progress in your naval career, you will often find that commands that do the "little" things well—salutes, rendering honors, and standing a taut quarterdeck watch—are often equally adept at the more complex, mission-oriented competencies as well. This is not a coincidence, and you will find that adherence to naval customs both reminds us of our heritage and provides an opportunity to correctly practice the little things that can make a big difference.

Saluting

Saluting is one of the basic expressions of respect that a junior shows to a senior officer. Very simply, you give a hand salute by raising your right hand sharply until your fingertips touch the edge of your cover just to the right of your right eye. Your upper arm should be parallel to the ground and your fingers should form a straight line to your elbow. Your thumb and fingers should be extended and together with your palm down. Finally, you conclude the salute by returning your hand fluidly down to your side.

Naval personnel render salutes only in uniform, when covered. If you are walking toward a senior officer, you give a salute ten to fifteen feet before you reach the officer and hold your salute until the senior returns it. As you salute, you are expected to give a short greeting ("good morning, sir [or ma'am]" before noon; "good afternoon, sir [or ma'am]" between 1200 and 1800; or "good evening, sir [or ma'am]" after 1800. In addition to returning your salute, the senior officer will customarily return your greeting; when you are saluted, you should always return the greeting as well as the salute.

Saluting on Board a Ship

Saluting on a ship incorporates a few additional customs. First, when you board a ship that is flying the national ensign, stop a few feet before you actually step on the ship, turn to and salute the flag (usually aft on the stern), and then pivot to salute the officer of the deck. When you leave the ship, give your salutes in reverse order—the OOD first, then the national ensign.

On a ship, if you are covered (usually outside the ship or on the bridge of the ship), you will salute a flag officer, the commanding officer, and visiting officers senior to the commanding officer each time you encounter

27

them. For other officers who are senior to you, render a salute during your first meeting with them during the day.

Greetings

Whether you are outdoors or indoors ashore (or inside a ship at sea), greetings are a very important part of the Navy's social and military fabric. Even in close quarters and after repeated encounters during the day, it is always acceptable and appropriate to look someone in the eye and greet them appropriately—regardless of whether they are senior or junior. Always greet a senior officer and never fail to positively respond to someone who has greeted you.

The Quarterdeck

Ships, and many shore commands, have a quarterdeck where watchstanders officially greet guests and control access to the broader command area. These areas almost always feature the national ensign and the Navy flag and should be traversed with respect. If you are entering the quarterdeck to visit the command, follow the directions of the officer or petty officer in charge—he or she is a direct representative of that command's commanding officer.

As a member of a command, the general custom is that you should avoid crossing the quarterdeck unless absolutely necessary. If you must do so, it is customary to ask permission of the OOD before crossing. Customs vary more broadly ashore, so be sure to ask another junior officer what is expected at your command.

National Anthem and Colors

While most of us have some familiarity with the basic customs related to the national anthem, as leaders who wear "the cloth of our nation" those who serve in uniform must get this custom right. When the national anthem is played and you are covered, face the national ensign if it is displayed, salute on the anthem's first note, and conclude your salute on the last note. If the flag is not displayed, face in the direction of the music instead. If you are in civilian clothes, stand at attention, place your right hand over your heart (vice saluting), and follow the same facing directions as for those in uniform. If you are wearing a ball cap or hat in civilian clothes, follow the same steps, but place the hat over your heart with your right hand.

On military installations, you will also encounter saluting requirements during morning and evening colors. Morning colors occurs at 0800 and is preceded by a short preparatory signal at 0755; it commences with the national anthem being played as the national ensign is raised. If you are outside, you are expected to face the national ensign and hold your salute during the national anthem. At sunset, evening colors is also preceded by a preparatory signal five minutes before taps is played as the national ensign is lowered. Once again, you maintain your salute during the playing of taps. If you are on base and in a car, you are expected to bring the car to rest until either morning or evening colors is completed, if it is safe to do so.

Wardroom Etiquette

On ships and submarines, wardrooms are the living room, dining room, and boardroom for most at-sea commands. These spaces often contain some of the ship's most valued possessions and are decorated more nicely than other working spaces on the ship. Not surprisingly, eating in the wardroom requires a little more thought than eating at an informal meal with your family or in a college cafeteria, but after a few meals the habits will come naturally:

★ Before you enter, leave your ball cap/cover outside the wardroom.
★ If a senior officer is already seated, request permission to join the mess.
★ Be on time for meals. For lunch and dinner, you will stand at your seat until the senior officer (usually the CO on small ships) invites everyone to sit down.
★ If you are late, request permission to join the mess late, but avoid making being late for meals a habit.
★ Avoid talking only about work and stick to topics of conversation that are appropriate for everyone at the table.
★ Treat every guest well. If you are seated near another shipmate's guest, be pleasant and attempt to include them in your conversation. If you bring guests, be sure to introduce them to the wardroom.
★ If you must leave the meal early, ask the senior person at the table to be excused.

Just as family customs vary, wardroom customs vary from ship to ship. In some wardrooms, meals are reminiscent of a happy family dinner while others are more formal. On some ships, coveralls and flight suits are acceptable, and other wardrooms require officers to change back into a more formal uniform. In some commands, holding meetings or doing individual work in the wardrooms are necessities whereas other ships strictly reserve the use of the wardroom for meals and a brief stop for coffee. Your best advice for navigating these issues in your wardroom will come from your shipmates who have preceded you. You, in turn, should help the next ensign who follows your arrival—they will have many of the same questions you do.

Interacting with Seniors

In a time and culture where the vast majority of employees refer to their bosses by first name, the military stands apart in the respect that our service accords to senior leaders. In addition to rendering a salute to a senior officer, there are several other courtesies you should follow:

★ If you are seated, stand up when senior leaders enter a room or space.

★ When you walk with the senior, stay to the right.

★ When entering a small boat, such as a barge or a liberty boat, you should enter first and leave last.

★ In automobiles, the senior should be offered the most desirable seat. Traditionally in a passenger car with a driver, this is the right window seat in the back, but in vans or personal cars, the senior may wish to take the front seat.

★ Always offer a seat to a senior.

★ Never leave a senior officer waiting.

★ Don't make excuses. When interacting with a senior in a professional setting, the five basic responses ("yes, sir"; "no, sir"; "aye, aye, sir"; "I'll find out, sir"; and "no excuse, sir") are superb guides to follow.

Ceremonies and Events You May Encounter

The variety and conduct of all naval ceremonies are too extensive to list in the confines of this small chapter, but there are a few core ceremonies that you can expect to see in your first year or two of service.

Change of Command

The high mobility of our profession virtually ensures that you will participate in one of these events as a junior officer. Command is the most valued of opportunities to serve in the U.S. Navy, so it is not surprising that we pause to formally recognize the turnover of command from one leader to another. The uniform for these events can range from service dress whites (choker whites) to wash khakis if the change of command is held at sea.

Because a change of command ceremony will often require effort in advance of the actual day's events, you may be tasked to provide support for the event. Your chief and you will also be expected to ensure that you and your Sailors are in the right uniform. As a junior officer, you may serve as an usher, a quarterdeck watchstander, or even a supervisor of a VIP parking area during the event. Regardless of your duties, give this ceremony the attention and respect it deserves.

Burial at Sea
If you are serving in an afloat command, your ship may play a role in providing those who have served their final resting place. These events very strictly follow the fleet guidance, including providing the families a videotape and letter describing their loved one's ceremony. Junior officers are often asked to stand in ranks or assist in the disposition of the deceased's ashes.

Ship Christenings and Commissionings
Bringing a ship to life from construction is one of the most challenging and memorable opportunities naval officers can experience in their professional life. Chapter 2 of *Command at Sea* contains a superb synopsis of this process, which usually includes a christening ceremony and culminates with a commissioning ceremony. The ship's christening occurs in the yard where the ship is being built and largely focuses on the namesake of the ship and the workers who have built it. If you are attached to the ship at the time of the christening, you will be expected to attend and will likely march with the other members of your command. The high point of this event occurs when the ship's sponsor breaks a bottle of champagne across the bow of the new ship.

The ship's commissioning, intended to mark the ship's formal entry into the fleet, usually takes place in a port other than the shipyard where the ship was built and occurs on a Friday or Saturday after a week's worth of activities in the commissioning port. This ceremony is almost always a formal event with participants in service dress whites or service dress blues with medals and swords. As a junior officer, you will likely participate in several extensive rehearsals to make sure that the ceremony—often attended by thousands—goes well, as well as cocktail parties to celebrate the occasion. Once again, it is essential to make sure that you and your Sailors have the right uniforms and understand their roles in each event.

Reenlistments and Retirements
As a new leader, you will likely have a Sailor who is reenlisting during your first year. In the Navy, these are important milestones as a Sailor commits an additional part of his life to the Navy. In most commands, reenlistments will involve a small ceremony, the oath of enlistment, and presentation of a few reenlistment benefits, all of which are frequently attended by the enlisting Sailor's family. If you are a division officer, you will not want to

Honors and ceremonies, such as this christening ceremony, are an integral part of the U.S. Navy's heritage. (Courtesy Bath Iron Works)

take these events lightly; make sure that they are well attended by your other Sailors and supported by the command. If your Sailor selects you as the reenlisting officer, view this as the honor it is and make sure you are prepared to administer the oath, ideally from memory to demonstrate the care and interest this event deserves.

You will occasionally encounter members of your command who are concluding their careers. These ceremonies are deeply valued in our service culture as they are the service's last opportunity to acknowledge that service member's service. If you are asked to support this event, do so to the best of your abilities because the retiring member has literally given the very best years of his or her adult life to the naval service.

Crossing the Line

Although this ceremony has evolved over the years, crossing the equator is a significant milestone in a ship's life. During this event, "shellbacks"—those who have crossed the equator before—oversee the induction of "polliwogs" into this sacred brotherhood. The ceremony concludes with the polliwogs being cleansed with salt water and deemed worthy by King Neptune and Davey Jones (the most senior shellbacks).

If you are "crossing the line" for the first time, your responsibilities will be limited to participating in the event and keeping your sense of humor. Although the vast majority of these ceremonies have been executed superbly, a very few over the years have descended into hazing or inappropriate treatment of some crew members. Rest assured that the senior members of your chain of command will be watching this carefully.

Dining In and Dining Out

In the Navy, a dining in traditionally refers to a wardroom-only event held on the ship or in a private dining area. Traditionally, officers dress in mess dress (or another formal uniform) and "the Vice," usually a seasoned member of the wardroom, serves as the host and closely monitors the behavior of all participants closely during the toasts, the meal, and the speaker's remarks.

As the ceremony nears completion, the Vice will assess "charges" to those members who have committed an etiquette or uniform infraction, with punishments varying from drinking "grog" to singing a song or telling a joke. Once the dinner begins, guests are not permitted to leave—even to go to the restroom—so be sure to watch your liquid intake. In some commands, dining ins now include the chief's mess.

Dining outs traditionally include the spouses or dates of the wardroom as well and almost always occur off-ship in a private dining room. Like the dining in, there is still a Vice who monitors and enforces good behavior and decorum, so be sure to share these customs with your spouse or date since you may be held "accountable" for his or her infractions! Once again, these events are generally conducted with a spirit of fun, so be sure to enjoy yourself. While the customs associated with these events may seem old-fashioned or an effort to prepare for, they are often some of the most memorable events of a tour, and they bind us to the generations of officers before us who participated in similar events.

Official Calls

In older books on military etiquette, authors spend considerable time on the mechanics of how an officer "makes a call" on a senior officer, usually his commanding officer. Fortunately, in today's Navy, this custom has been replaced by two relatively simple events. First, you will almost always meet with your commanding officer within the first week or so of arriving at your new command. In small at-sea commands, this may be the first of many encounters with your CO. On larger commands, it may be some time before you meet the captain again. In either case, you will want to be prepared to talk about your background and goals you have for your time as a member of the captain's team. Additionally, you will want to make sure that you are in a good uniform, well groomed, and ready to engage the CO positively—first impressions can last a long time.

The second component of this process is usually a "Hail and Farewell," covered more extensively in chapter 4 of this book. This social gathering, often hosted at an officer's home, will collectively serve to welcome those who have newly arrived and bid farewell to those leaving the command. Generally, hail and farewells occur every two to three months and can serve to be one of the social rituals that you will remember fondly as you grow older.

While the custom of "calling" on senior officers has evolved significantly, if you are in an afloat command this custom still survives for your commanding officer when visiting other ports. As a junior officer on duty, you may be detailed to escort or drive your CO on such visits which usually last fifteen to thirty minutes, often involve coffee or tea, and conclude with an exchange of a small gift. If you are directed to assist, make sure that you are in the right uniform, are well groomed, and pay attention—in a few short years, you may be a young commanding officer doing the same thing.

Foreign Customs

Although it might seem hard to believe after reviewing the number of ceremonies in this chapter, our military is a reflection of the informality of American culture. Overseas, most military cultures are much more observant and connected to the ritual of social customs. If you anticipate having to play a role in ceremonies or calls involving international services or international locations, a thorough review of that nation's customs and history is warranted.

On a ship, you will be able to draw upon the experience of those who have served overseas and ensure that you attend the "port brief" that customarily occurs after a ship pulls into a foreign port. Through e-mail at sea, your command will also be able to reach back to protocol experts off the ship to make sure that you are abiding by the customs that will represent you and the U.S. Navy most appropriately to your hosts.

Conclusion

Naval customs provide a common framework for naval personnel to interact and work well together. More importantly, these customs also embody the tradition and core values that are integral to the naval service's heritage. While these customs may warrant additional review and effort, cherish them—they help to create the foundation of our naval service, binding together naval generations past, present, and future.

★ 4 ★

SOCIAL ETIQUETTE

D
r. Robert Fulgham wrote a popular book in the eighties, *All I Really Need to Know I Learned in Kindergarten*, that emphasized that most of the basics of human interaction haven't changed since kindergarten—and this certainly applies to social etiquette. Although the word "etiquette" often evokes stiff, formal dinners or the rules that prepare one to participate in such an event, the reality is that etiquette provides a framework of consideration, respect, and consistency for us to interact with others. There may be some rules of etiquette that seem old-fashioned, but you will always be well served if you approach social dealings with the intent to be respectful of others' feelings.

The principal reference on etiquette for the naval officer is *Service Etiquette* by Oretha Schwartz, available at most U.S. Navy uniform shops on base. Although the rise of e-mail and a general loosening of formality, among other things, have changed our social landscape since *Service Etiquette* was last updated, it remains a very valuable and comprehensive reference. This chapter will not serve as a substitute for a comprehensive guide on etiquette but will aim to provide an overview of the basics that pertain to the majority of social issues you will encounter as a newly commissioned naval officer.

If it has been a while since you have reviewed social customs for writing "thank you" notes and tipping a waiter or baggage handler, consider investing in a basic etiquette book. While your social life at college or your prior enlisted experience likely comprised a series of informal get-togethers and social events, you will encounter a broader range of social activities as a naval officer. Of many etiquette books available, one of the best known and accepted versions is *Emily Post on Etiquette* written by Elizabeth L. Post. Regardless of which book you choose, take heart that most of these books cover similar ground, and most advice aligns fairly closely from book to book. Be sure to pick a book that you find readable and user-friendly—a book that is too large or intimidating for everyday use will probably just sit on your shelf.

General Socializing and Entertaining

One aspect of naval life that officers usually remember long after their service is the fun they have had socializing with friends in the Navy. Although socializing in the Navy is not as formal as depicted in some World War II–era movies or as raucous as portrayed in movies such as *Top Gun*, it will likely be more structured than what you may have experienced in college or in your previous service as an enlisted Sailor.

In many ways, the social transition you make from your previous life to your social life as an officer will be very similar to what a young professional experiences after leaving college for his or her first workplace. There will still be time for you to socialize with your closest friends in an environment and style that are comfortable for you, but you will also find that your social group will very naturally expand to include the people you work with. Socializing with coworkers is common in most professions, and many who share your profession will often share other interests as well.

Yet because you will live, travel, and operate with your coworkers, if your first naval job is in a deployable command, socializing often takes on greater significance for officers and their families. While some "career strategists" may assert that socializing within the wardroom is critical to your success and must be carefully managed, this is more urban legend than fact. Certainly there will be some social commitments that come with being a part of a naval command, but in many ways they will be no more demanding than what would be expected of a member of a civilian executive team where meeting with clients and coworkers is an expected part of the job.

More important than any perceived professional benefit, the reality is that being in the Navy will be much better when you have friends with whom to share the experience. With this in mind, investing in your naval experience by participating in social events—whether they include grabbing an informal meal or participating in an organized event such as a command dining out—will only make your broader life richer.

Some general advice: Be yourself and do what you enjoy. For most new ensigns, you can take comfort that you have had more social experiences that will be similar to those you will encounter in the Navy than you might think. During most commissioning tracks, officer candidates and midshipmen participate in a range of social events that are representative of some of the social events you will see in the military. That notwithstanding, you

Not all social events in the military are formal. Here a wardroom enjoys a wetting down ceremony celebrating a new officer's promotion. (Courtesy USS *Stockdale*)

have now entered the working world as a junior executive in the military, so it is worth giving thought to the social side of your life.

Meals

Reviewing general table manners will be a worthwhile endeavor if most of your meals have recently been consumed in a college cafeteria or another informal eating environment. Rest assured that most of the people you are dealing with were not raised in a country club or formal dining environment either, so reviewing table manners before a formal meal is something that many of us have to do.

Whether you review Schwarz's *Service Etiquette* or a more general etiquette book, the basics remain the same. As you face your plate, remember the acronym "BMW," like the car, which corresponds to "bread, meal, water." This will remind you that you will use the bread plate on the left side of your dinner plate and drink from the glasses on your right. Place your napkin in your lap and never tuck it into your neck or lap. When you leave the table, place the napkin to the left of your plate (not crumpled or refolded, just loosely folded). It is customary to pass things in a counterclockwise direction. Avoid reaching for things and instead ask someone closer to you to pass the item to you. Just as your parents may have reminded you as a child, sitting up straight, chewing with your mouth closed, and not speaking with your mouth full are basic rules to follow.

Hosting or Organizing an Event

At some point in your early career, you may want to host your own social event and include some of your wardroom counterparts in addition to having a few friends over to watch a football game or a movie. You will not be expected to equal an event that has been hosted by a senior officer, but a few guidelines will assist you in making the event a success.

Keep Things Simple

If you are hosting an actual command or departmental event, keeping things simple is fine. Many naval events, even full wardroom social functions, are potluck, so your guests will not find it odd at all if your invitation requests that they bring a side dish or another item to your home if they choose to participate. In today's environment, you are certainly not required to provide alcohol at an event you host, but if you do, make sure that you have nonalcoholic beverages as well.

Be Inclusive

If you are hosting a party or an event that can easily include more participants (as opposed to a dinner where space will limit whom you can include), try to be inclusive with the members of the wardroom. Although certain activities will dictate limited numbers, if you are going to host an event that might lend itself to a broader group, consider widening the invitation.

Although being inclusive is important, you are certainly allowed to socialize with one or two friends or couples from the ship. Going to dinner or participating in a common interest often naturally limits the size of a group for a given event. As with any other group of people, you will be drawn to some peers more naturally than others, but avoid setting a social pattern that could be perceived as a clique. There are few things more divisive in an otherwise good wardroom than the development of cliques among officers, or their spouses.

Consider Activities beyond Your Home

If the size of your home does not allow you to entertain in great numbers, you may want to consider organizing an outing somewhere else. As with friendships outside the Navy, interests in sports, music, movies, or even a certain type of food (barbecue, ethnic food, etc.) provide the common ground that has often initiated lifelong friendships. The Navy's morale, welfare, and recreation (MWR) program provides you the opportunity to try new activities that may become lifelong hobbies. Many officers have developed a lifelong love of fishing, golf, tennis, or sailing after trying these activities for the first time as a junior officer. While you should not feel compelled to pick up an activity merely because your boss enjoys it, if you are genuinely interested in an activity and have been invited to participate, give it a try.

Fun Things to Do

In addition to organizing social events for your own enjoyment, you may be asked to come up with an activity for your wardroom, office, or department to participate in. Here are a few activities to consider. Many of these may in fact be supported or discounted by the MWR center on your nearest naval installation:

★ Attending regional festivals
★ Eating out as a group at a gourmet or ethnic restaurant
★ Hosting a football party
★ Spending a day at the beach for a volleyball party
★ Running a 5K or 10K as a wardroom or command
★ Visiting a museum or an art exhibit
★ Visiting national and state parks or historic sites together
★ Attending a concert or play
★ Attending minor league baseball games or other athletic events
★ Visiting comedy clubs
★ Going deep sea fishing
★ Performing a community service project as a group

Not every one of these events will be a good fit for every group—particularly a larger, "all-wardroom" event—but most people enjoy and appreciate events that offer variety and a departure from the norm.

Responding to Invitations

During your first tour as an ensign, you will almost certainly receive an invitation to a social event hosted by another officer, often someone senior to you. Remember to respond in a timely and appropriate manner to those invitations. Usually an invitation will indicate if the host expects you to reply and will provide an e-mail address, phone number, or response card to do so. If a response is requested, respond with a "yes" or "no" via the manner described on the invitations (unless the invitation indicates regrets only).

If you remember the notion that most etiquette is based on consideration, respect, and consistency, it should be obvious why responding promptly is so important. On a practical level, your hosts will want to have a good idea of how many folks will be coming so they can appropriately prepare for an event. Additionally, there is nothing more dispiriting for hosts than being left to wonder how many guests will come to an event they have prepared extensively for. Remembering the Golden Rule and thinking about how you would want to be treated if you were hosting an event should guide your actions.

If you do accept an invitation, it is always nice to offer to bring something to support the host's effort. If, after inquiring what you can bring, the host replies that he or she does not need any assistance, a small token of thanks such as a bottle of wine or flowers will always be appreciated. Remember that once you have accepted an invitation, make every effort to attend. This is the considerate thing to do and points to your general efforts to keep your promises and commitments.

Social and Personal Conduct as an Officer

As a commissioned officer you represent the Navy twenty-four hours a day, seven days a week. This may sound overly dramatic, or even burdensome, but it is unfailingly true. Even if you are on leave or off duty, your good personal conduct or your failure to meet these standards will reflect on your command, your shipmates, and our Navy. Simply put, you will want your conduct to be such that your parents—or the parents of your Sailors—would be proud.

Although the vast majority of young officers conduct themselves admirably, even the most upright people can lose their way. Most shortfalls in conduct stem from a lack of judgment rather than a lack of character, and nothing accelerates this process more than the abuse of alcohol. Remember that how you dress, the events you attend, and the businesses you patronize also can reflect back on the Navy. None of this means that you will not be able to have a good time or let your hair down a bit, but always keep your role as an ambassador for the naval service in mind as you make decisions related to your social and personal conduct.

Hail and Farewells

One of the most common events you will encounter as junior officer is the Hail and Farewell—a social event dedicated to welcoming new additions to the officers' community at your command and providing a fitting sendoff for those who are departing. The form and tone of these events vary based on warfare community and individual commands, so take the time to ask a more experienced officer at your command what you should expect.

In its most basic form, the Hail and Farewell begins with an informal meal or light fare, proceeds to the commanding officer welcoming the new additions and their significant others, and the wardroom recognizing those who are leaving. This recognition can take the form of sincere appreciation, gentle ribbing, or a downright roast—make sure you understand what the custom is at your command and recognize that, as a new person with limited time at your command, you will likely not be expected to make many remarks.

If you are bringing your spouse or a guest to the event, work hard to introduce that person to some of the other officers and guests. If spouses and other guests are included, make an effort to keep any remarks or gifts tasteful. These events are one of the primary ways wardrooms bond outside of the command, but misreading the climate or inadvertently hurting someone's feelings with a comment that was intended to be funny is a pitfall to avoid.

Thank You Notes

Writing letters and notes has become a bit of a lost art with the advent of e-mail, but thank you notes are a social custom that has not been replaced with an electronic substitute just yet. If a senior officer has hosted you for dinner, it is always appropriate to thank the host for his or her efforts with a note of thanks. These notes do not have to be long, but they should be sincere and written with specificity so they do not read like a form letter. Remember to pick a thank you note card that is both an appropriate representative of who you are and suitable for the person receiving it. A white or cream note card with your initials or a conservative picture on the front would be a good choice if you have never shopped for stationery before. Regardless, sending a note of thanks to someone who has hosted you for a meal or been kind to you in another way is a courtesy that will never go out of style.

Civilian Clothing

Just as you will want to be in the right uniform at a military event, we all feel our best when we are dressed appropriately in street clothes as well.

If you have not had a chance to purchase a suit yet, this is probably the right time to do so. A conservative dark suit for more formal events and a high quality blue blazer for less formal occasions would be good additions for a young male officer's wardrobe, and female officers should look to buy clothing that is appropriate for more formal events as well. For young officers, all of these purchases will likely represent a substantial expense in light of your limited budget, but remember that a few high-quality, conservatively styled items will provide you with the best return on your clothing investment over the long run.

While the vast majority of your events will likely be ones where khakis and a polo shirt or button-down will be the right choice for men and dress slacks or a skirt for women, there will be times when having a suit or blazer available will allow you to more comfortably participate in a social event. If you are in a command that deploys, you will definitely want to bring a civilian suit or blazer along with some of your less formal liberty attire (female officers will want to bring the appropriate equivalent to a suit or blazer for men).

In many other parts of the world, dining can be more formal and having a sport coat or nicer dress will make you more comfortable. Events in more conservative regions of the world may require females to wear a shawl or jacket rather than a sleeveless outfit. Additionally, you may be invited to an optional event or two that would require nicer clothing. These opportunities to dine with a local dignitary or business leaders are often very positive, memorable experiences that you will not want to miss because you left your sport coat or nice dress at home prior to deployment.

Most of the events you participate in, however, will not require a coat and tie or a more formal dress. Regardless of where you are going, represent the Navy well. Ripped, suggestive, or revealing clothing must be avoided, and although flip-flops are fine at a beach party, for example, they are not a good bet for your first wardroom function at the commanding officer's house.

Introductions

The Navy is not overly formal regarding introductions in general, but because this is a very mobile profession, most naval leaders will expect you to introduce yourself and the person who may be accompanying you to an event—they are looking forward to meeting you! In many ways, because this is such a standard custom, you will quickly find yourself becoming very comfortable with introductions, and you can expect to assimilate much more quickly into a social setting than you would in a civilian environment.

The mechanics of a simple introduction are not that difficult. A simple, "Commander Jones, I would like to introduce you to my friend, John Smith," works just fine. The general rules of introductions are that a junior person is introduced to a senior, a younger person to someone older, and, if seniority is not an issue, females are introduced to males. If you remember to mention the senior person first, the rest of the introduction is easy—"Admiral Smith . . . I would like you to meet my wife, Katherine Jackson."

Tipping

While the standard tip for a waiter is 15–20 percent for a sit-down meal in the United States, there are a number of other services where a tip is often expected. At hotels, it is customary to tip bellhops one dollar per bag, with the same going to skycaps if they help you with your bags at the airport. On many naval bases, baggers at the commissary (the on-base grocery store) are often paid largely from small tips—obviously different from most civilian food shopping experiences. For barbershops and beauty shops both on base and off base, tipping customs are relatively similar—15–20 percent of the price of the service. For taxi drivers, tip 15 percent of the overall fare.

Internationally, tipping customs vary widely, so it is worth checking with those who have lived in a country for a while or refer to any number of travel books. If you are part of a deployed command, you will often receive an entering port brief where local customs are discussed by those who reside in the nation you are visiting. Those briefing you will be an excellent source of advice on tipping and, more broadly, other social customs in the country you are visiting.

Conclusion

The discussion of etiquette may initially seem contrived or stiff, but the intent is the exact opposite. By showing consideration, respect, and consistency in the way you approach your social interaction, you are actually creating a framework that will enhance your ability to socially engage others and be comfortable and confident. Most officers find the naval profession's code of social ethics to be one of the great features of naval life and one that creates a foundation for friendships that can last a lifetime. Although this small chapter will not make you a protocol expert, remembering the watchwords "consideration," "respect," and "consistency" will serve you well as you embark on your naval career.

★ 5 ★

LEAVE, LIBERTY, AND TRAVEL

Leave and liberty are subjects near and dear to any Sailor's heart, and they will be to you, too. The old recruiting ad slogan that Sailors "join the Navy, to see the world" is often quite true, and even in this age of heightened force protection, the opportunity to travel is still a very attractive feature of the naval profession. Even if your next journey is from your apartment to your workplace, it will be worthwhile to review the Navy's policies on leave, liberty, and travel as you manage your own travels and monitor the liberty and leave of your Sailors.

Leave

All service members have a right to leave. Leave is a formally granted paid "vacation" that will only be interrupted in extraordinary circumstances. You will accumulate 2.5 days of leave per month of active service (30 days per year), and you can carry a maximum of 75 days across a fiscal year. In other words, if you had 90 days of unused leave "on the books" on 1 October, you would lose 15 of those days and would begin accumulating 2.5 days per month again until the next fiscal year. Of course, if you regularly use your leave, you will keep the total accumulated number of days remaining below 75 at the end of the fiscal year and will never lose any. (Note: Traditionally, naval members have been able to carry 60 days of leave at the end of the fiscal year, but this has been raised to 75 through 2010.) Under exceptional circumstances, such as a family emergency, leave that puts you in a negative leave balance state will be granted as long as you have enough obligated service left to "work off" the negative leave balance at the rate of 2.5 days per month, but this exception is managed very carefully.

Leave requests are made on a standard leave request/authorization form, which is routed through your chain of command for approval or disapproval. Except in the case of emergency, leave requests should be routed well in advance. The command duty officer, officer of the deck, or admin

While Sailors may join the Navy to see the world, Navy leaders also make it a better place. Here ENS James Zumwalt makes a drawing for a child living in an orphanage in Vietnam. (U.S. Navy, MC2 John Beeman)

officer will sign your leave papers at the bottom, indicating the dates and times you actually checked out on leave and returned. After returning from leave, be sure to turn the completed leave chit into the admin office.

Emergency leave is granted under special circumstances such as the illness or death of an immediate family member. An important point, however, is that emergency leave is not free. It will still be charged against your leave balance, but it sometimes offers benefits such as priority placement on military transportation or reduced prices on commercial airline tickets.

Liberty

Liberty is the time you have after work until the start of the next work day. In the Navy, this will vary with workload and operational schedule. You can expect to be granted liberty at the end of a normal workday unless you have duty. Being on liberty does not mean you are free from the Navy's regulations and expectations: quite to the contrary, you are *always* subject to the rules and regulations of the Navy and your command.

Liberty for enlisted Sailors is often a more formal process because most at-sea commands observe set work hours and muster times, but officers often have a little more latitude in managing their own liberty. Despite this extra flexibility, you will be expected to be ready and prepared for officer's

45

call and quarters in the morning, and usually your own self-imposed schedule will be far more demanding than anything formally published in the plan of the day.

Travel

During your career, you will likely travel in an official capacity both individually and as part of a group. You will also be able to take advantage of various opportunities to travel in an unofficial capacity on military transport for personal leisure.

Official Travel

Much of the traveling you will do in your naval career will be defined as temporary additional duty, universally known as TAD. In your first few years of service, your most likely form of TAD will be for schools and instruction less than six months in length. You may be required to travel individually or in small groups in support of your command's mission (attending conferences, visiting subunits, cross-training opportunities, and visiting sites in industry). Travel in this case may be on military aircraft and vehicles, or you may be issued a commercial airline ticket. In either case, you will be entitled to certain monetary allowances, which you will receive after filing a travel claim, described below.

Travel allowances. The Joint Federal Travel Regulations (JFTR) govern all Department of Defense (DoD) travel. Usually you can expect to be paid a per diem rate sufficient to pay for accommodations and meals when on TAD travel. You will also be reimbursed for certain other expenses such as tolls and taxies, if used for official business. When traveling by commercial air, you may be entitled to a rental car, but be sure this is spelled out on your orders before you travel.

Frequent travelers are issued a government-provided credit card to secure lodging, pay for meals, car rental (if it has been preapproved), and so on. Over the years, misuse of government credit cards has resulted in very tight restrictions on who the cards can be issued to and what they can be used to purchase. If you are curious, you can dig further into the JFTR at https://secureapp2.hqda.pentagon.mil/perdiem/trvlregs.html; otherwise, talk to your admin office about exactly what you are entitled to.

Travel claims. After completion of travel, you will need to submit a travel claim to your admin office to get reimbursed for your expenses. After your local personnel support detachment (PSD) processes your claim, the appropriate sum of money will be deposited directly into your bank account.

After an extended period of travel, such as during a permanent change of station (PCS) move for you and your family, submitting a travel claim can be fairly complicated. Be sure to keep all of your receipts for lodging, rental cars, plane tickets, and any other expenses over seventy-five dollars.

Traveling in uniform. When traveling within the United States, you may be required to travel in uniform if you are part of a command-sponsored group. During most domestic travel situations, wearing civilian clothes will be the more practical choice. You travel in uniform, you will usually be in the uniform of the day (either dress blues or summer whites), but CNT "dress" khakis are also acceptable. Outside of the United States, you will always be required to wear civilian clothes when using commercial transportation, for force-protection reasons. If you are flying on a military transport, you may be required to wear a uniform; make sure you check ahead with the military air terminal you will be departing from.

Unofficial Travel
Aside from normal leave and liberty, one of the great benefits of military life is the chance to explore foreign lands. Your ship or squadron may visit overseas locations, or you may simply decide to take advantage of a military transport "hop" for leave in an international city or tourist destination.

Travel associated with normal leave and liberty within the United States. Every service member is entitled to leave and liberty, and you will no doubt want to take advantage of the opportunity to travel away from your home port or base. There are a few rules you should keep in mind: Any absence outside of the normal workday usually requires an approved "special request" chit. An absence greater than ninety-six hours will require the member to take formal leave.

In addition to these general rules, local commands may have restrictions on how far you can travel from home base without submitting a special request chit or leave papers. Check with your department head on this issue. The "managing your division's leave and liberty" section below presents some considerations for safe travel that apply equally to your Sailors and to you—always keep in mind that in almost every year in recent history, more Sailors have been killed or injured on leave and liberty than while at work.

Overseas travel. When traveling overseas you will generally need to submit a leave request. It is also a good idea to give an itinerary and list of contact numbers to your department head before you depart so she can track you down if needed. Many local commanders overseas have rules on the minimum size of a travel party ("buddy rules") and a detailed list of off-limits locations. Check with your anti-terrorism/force protection officer to see if any of these rules apply, or if you need to be briefed on the local terrorism threat (the more "exotic" the location you intend to visit, the more likely you will need to complete a training session). In many cases you will be required to prepare an individual force protection and travel plan even if your travel is for pleasure.

Just as when you are at home, you are a representative of both your country and the Navy when you travel abroad. Respect local customs, dress and act appropriately, and avoid confrontations with the locals. If you do find yourself in trouble, contact your command and the nearest U.S. military facility or consulate as soon as possible.

Space-A travel. As a member of the military, you are entitled to take advantage of military air transport for free (or nearly free) travel, a terrific way to use your off-duty time to see the world. For the most part, this means using the formal Air Force Air Mobility Command (AMC) Space Available system. A word of caution: "Space available" means exactly that. If there is a seat available on an aircraft bound for your destination, you will get it, but if a higher priority passenger shows up just before departure, you could find yourself scrambling to find alternative (and expensive) transportation. Aircraft may also be diverted or delayed with no notice. Always give yourself a time cushion when traveling Space-A, and make sure you have an alternative way home if the worst happens. For more on using AMC Space-A, take a look at these websites:

★ Air Mobility Command: http://www.amc.af.mil/questions/topic.asp ?id=380
★ NAS Norfolk Passenger Terminal: http://www.airtermnorva.navy.mil/ Travel.htm

Managing Your Division's Leave and Liberty

Leave and liberty are subjects that loom large in the daily life of your Sailors. You will be faced with many requests for special liberty and leave, which you will have to balance against workload, operations, and command policy. Up front, you should know that a good leader knows when to say "no." The flip side of this coin is that a good leader should also know when to fight for a request that warrants approval. This section will present some tips on how to handle your division's time off.

Normal Leave

Normal leave generally falls into one of two categories: command-wide stand-down periods and individual leave. The first category, command-wide stand-down leave, will occur on a designated period over a holiday or after a deployment. The usual practice is to divide the stand-down period in half and allow the crew to take leave during one half or the other. Your job here is to make sure that there are enough people around during each period to carry on with routine work and man watches (building a bar chart with each member of your division down the side and the date they will take leave across the top is one useful way to visualize the situation). Remember to keep an eye on your Sailors' leave balance—allowing someone to attain a negative leave balance should be approached with caution. Finally, you will inevitably have to deal with requests that do not match up with designated leave periods. These requests may not merit an automatic "no" but must be viewed in context with the ship's needs and fairness to your other Sailors.

The second category of normal leave, individual leave, can often require a little more skill to manage. Notionally, operational commands normally permit 10 percent of an organization to take leave during normal import periods. Before checking the "yes" box and passing the chit up the chain of command, you must consider divisional workload, the command's operational schedule, the member's leave balance, and command policies. You will also have to consider if the leave applicant has a unique or critical skill that the command cannot afford to lose for that period of time. No one can tell you how to react for every case, but you must balance the individual's needs against the impact on your division and the command and be prepared to articulate your decision.

Emergency Leave

Many of the same considerations for ordinary leave apply to the decision to grant emergency leave, but the thought process will be biased in favor of the individuals' needs if they meet the criteria for emergency leave. It will be a rare circumstance where leave is not granted in the case of a genuine emergency involving the immediate family of one of your Sailors. Of course, what constitutes a "genuine emergency" is often in the eye of the beholder—you will no doubt experience situations during your career where you doubt if the "emergency" in question really merits granting leave, especially if your unit is deployed overseas. In these gray areas, seek the advice of your chief or department head.

One way to confirm that an emergency is genuine is to request an "AMCROSS" message. The American Red Cross works closely with all military bases by helping to confirm emergencies (often by consulting with a physician) and transmitting a message or calling the command directly. Most medical facilities that deal with military patients will be familiar with this process, but in some cases you may need to have the Sailor contact his family on the scene to get things rolling. Another valuable resource in this case is the command ombudsman, who is specifically trained to deal with situations like these.

Coincident with processing the emergency leave request, you will need to ensure that adequate travel arrangements are made and that the Sailor has sufficient funds to get home. Consult with your command master chief on this issue—many commands have a small emergency fund, or can expedite processing of a loan from Navy–Marine Corps Relief Society. For more on Navy Relief, which assists service members in need with loans and grants, see the Navy–Marine Corps Relief Society Web site: www. nmcrs.org.

Liberty

As a general rule, you should seek to provide the daily time off for your Sailors that is consistent with your command's liberty policies. While you never want to hold them on the ship or at work unnecessarily, you will want to balance the notion of maximizing liberty with the need to do more than merely complete the minimal jobs necessary to keep your organization afloat.

One thing that will quickly be apparent to you is that there is always something to do in the Navy. All of us value our free time, but you must always keep mission accomplishment uppermost in your mind. Your command may or may not have a strict policy on liberty hours; if not, talk this issue over with your chief and your department head. No matter what the policy, you must be prepared to manage liberty appropriately to meet an often challenging work load. As always, keep your boss informed.

Depending on the operational tempo of your command, there may be times where your Sailors will desire liberty during the day to take care of a particular need or participate in an event during the day, such as serving as a class parent. While your chief and you will certainly want to support worthwhile requests if your command schedule can support it, you will also want to make sure that your Sailors are not habitually asking for time off during the workday to accomplish items that they could do on their own time. As in many leadership experiences, these decisions require a sense of balance between the needs of your Sailors and the needs of your command.

Liberty normally expires in the morning around 0700, at which time your division will turn in a muster report, accounting for all hands.

Sometimes—especially when overseas—liberty will expire at an unusual time, such as midnight. In these cases, good division officers will be up and about to make sure everybody in their divisions has made it back to the ship on time and in good shape.

Special Liberty

Special liberty is granted for specific reasons during normal working hours, for periods of twenty-four to ninety-six hours. It is approved though the process of routing a special request chit up the chain of command. Local policies vary, but most units give authority to division officers to grant up to twenty-four hours of special liberty while longer periods (up to a maximum of ninety-six hours) must be granted further up the chain. As with all special requests, any chit that is marked "no" must go all the way up the chain of command for final disposition.

Safety Considerations

Motor vehicle accidents are the leading cause of death and serious injury in the Navy. Most leave and liberty involve travel, often over long distances in varying weather. As a good division officer, you should pay close attention to your people's travel plans, and spend some time talking about making smart choices. You should also consider vehicle safety inspections and requiring a "trip plan," especially for your younger Sailors. The Navy Safety Center Web site has examples of vehicle inspection check sheets, trip plans, and a host of tips on driver and travel safety: http://www.safety center.navy.mil/ashore/motorvehicle/toolbox/default.htm.

Conclusion

Leave and liberty are vital to the well-being of you and your Sailors. As a newly commissioned officer, you will spend a considerable amount of your energy managing leave and liberty for the Sailors who work for you. On occasion, you will have to make some hard calls while trying to balance the needs of individual Sailors with broader mission accomplishment. Make sure you understand local policies, communicate with your boss, and always be honest with your Sailors. Even though you will not be able to make every single Sailor happy every time, by taking the steps outlined in this chapter you will be well on your way to consistently managing this important aspect of naval life.

★ 6 ★

PAY AND BENEFITS

The Navy is a large, complex organization, so it should not be surprising that the structure of naval pay and benefits warrants some review. In addition to understanding your own compensation, as a leader you will also need to be equipped to provide counsel to your Sailors when they need it.

Pay

Your monthly paycheck—which includes basic pay, special pays, and allowances—is dispersed to your bank account twice a month, in two relatively equal amounts. You will also receive various one-time disbursements for things like travel and moving expenses. Finally, most officers will receive periodic bonuses for committing to further service. This section will briefly discuss each of these pay types to get you oriented, and provide some Web sites for further information.

Basic Pay

Basic pay is set by law based on your pay grade (rank) and years of service. You will receive a pay raise when you are promoted and with every two years of completed service. Each year, Congress adjusts the pay tables with an across-the-board raise to account for inflation (often around 2.5 to 3 percent) and may target certain pay grades for slightly higher raises to influence retention. Currently, the officer pay table runs from zero to forty years of service and from pay grades O-1 (ensign) to O-10 (admiral). The Web address below will take you to the current pay table at the Defense Finance Accounting Service (DFAS) military pay site. Click on "Military Pay Tables," then go to the year you are looking for: http://www.dod.mil/ dfas/militarypay.html.

Special Pays

Special pays come in many varieties. Some of the most common include sea pay, flight pay, and sub pay. Flight pay and submarine pay are for aircraft crew members and officers assigned to submarine duty, respectively. Officers assigned to seagoing commands are eligible for sea pay as well. Imminent danger pay is for service in designated geographic regions such as the Middle East, and hazardous duty pay is received when involved in certain hazardous activities such as flight deck operations. Dollar amounts for each of these pays are available at the current fiscal year Web site cited above. For detailed eligibility requirements, you may consult the Department of Defense comptroller's site: http://www.dtic.mil/comptroller/ fmr/07a/index.html.

For a user-friendly explanation of special pays, visit one of the commercial Web sites that cater to the military, such as www.military.com or www.militarytimes.com. As always, when it comes to pay, talk to your disbursing officer or local personnel support detachment (PSD) if you have questions.

Allowances

The final part of your monthly paycheck is made up various allowances. Officers will receive a basic allowance for subsistence (BAS) to pay for meals (note that officers will pay for their meals even while assigned to a ship), and a family separation allowance (FSA) while deployed, if they have dependents. Basic allowance for housing (BAH) covers housing costs and varies depending on location, pay grade, and marital status. BAH charts for each geographic area are available at the Web site below by typing in the zip code of the area you are interested in: http://perdiem.hqda.pentagon .mil/perdiem/.

Bonus Pay

Most officers who choose to serve past their initial service obligation will receive annual bonuses in exchange for agreeing to continue to serve. In the case of nuclear power officers and special warfare officers, these bonuses can be substantial. Rules vary greatly by community, so talk to a mentor or your detailer for specifics. Skimming the Bureau of Naval Personnel (BUPERS) Web site for your officer community may also yield some answers: http://www.npc.navy.mil/Officer/.

Notes on Taxation

Not all of your pay is taxable. The rule of thumb is that compensation that has "pay" in its name is taxable while anything that is an "allowance" is nontaxable. Another nuance is that pay received in a war or "hazardous" zone is nontaxable up to a certain amount. The nontaxable portion rule is rather complicated for officers—any pay above what the command master chief of the Navy (roughly, an E-9 over forty years of service on the pay chart) would receive is taxable.

Bonus payments are taxed based on the month you receive them, so they would be fully taxed under normal circumstances and only taxed beyond whatever an E-9's pay is if they are received while serving in a combat zone. The areas that qualify for "tax free" are set by the Department of Defense, and eligibility is based on the member spending at least one day of any given month in a designated zone. For the last decade and a half, the waters of the Persian Gulf have been designated as a tax-free area. The supply officer or disbursing officer at your command will be well versed in these issues if you have any questions.

Managing Your Pay

The Navy allows service members to manage certain aspects of their pay through a Defense Finance Accounting Service (DFAS)–supported Web site known as MyPay. The MyPay site allows you to view your monthly leave and earnings statement (LES), which gives a detailed account of all monthly pays, deductions (for things such as taxes and allotments), and your accumulated leave days. You should examine your LES monthly, especially if you note an unexpected increase or decrease in pay. Other functions available on the MyPay site include:

★ Starting, stopping, or modifying a savings allotment or a monthly allotment to a dependent
★ Setting up or modifying the account where your pay is deposited ("direct deposit")
★ Purchasing a savings bond
★ Changing your federal or state tax withholding status
★ Obtaining a copy of your annual W-2 form
★ Viewing the allotment of monthly pay to the Thrift Savings Plan (more on TSP later)
★ Tracking the disposition of any travel claims you have submitted in the last 180 days
★ The MyPay site is password protected. You can sign up at https://mypay.dfas.mil/mypay.aspx.

If you run into problems with your pay (not unheard of in the naval service), you will need to talk to your local PSD or to the command PSD liaison representative (PLR). If you have to work directly with PSD, your command should have a designated customer service representative to help you, but quite often you can resolve problems through the PLR in your unit's admin office.

Pay and Your Sailors

In your role as a leader, you will encounter Sailors with a wide range of financial backgrounds and knowledge, running the gamut from those with a significant portfolio and a solid investment plan to the newly married eighteen-year-old who has never filed a tax return or learned to balance a checkbook. Those who are most vulnerable often fall prey to easy credit and unscrupulous lenders, so the Navy spends considerable time trying to equip its Sailors with the knowledge to avoid these traps. You will play a significant role in these efforts, and when problems do occur, you will need to be involved as well.

Fortunately, the Servicemembers' Civil Relief Act has reduced the prevalence of these unfair lending practices in recent years. Nevertheless, it is always a good idea to discuss these issues with your Sailors regularly to help them avoid these financial pitfalls. This is especially important for Sailors in technical ratings. Uncontrolled and unpaid debts can prevent Sailors from obtaining or maintaining access to classified information.

Guiding Your Sailors

A little advance effort can go a long way toward helping your Sailors avoid financial problems. Take the time to informally talk to your troops about making smart financial decisions and avoiding the pitfalls of too much debt. Also, consider scheduling formal divisional training using the command financial specialist (CFS) or outside experts to provide instruction. For younger Sailors, or for those who appear to be headed toward financial trouble, get them one-on-one counseling with the CFS or at the local Fleet and Family Support Center (FFSC).

The FFSC in each U.S. Navy home port provides excellent financial counseling geared both to individuals in trouble and to helping Sailors and their families build a secure financial future. In addition to providing individual counseling, each FFSC periodically offers free classes on such subjects as the dangers of payday loans and easy credit, car-buying strategies, retirement planning, savings and investments, and identity theft awareness. Below is the main Web site for the FFSC, but search for the site associated with your local FFSC to get class details and contact numbers: https://www.nffsp.org/skins/nffsp/home.aspx.

Sailors in Financial Distress

Financial burdens can impact the day-to-day performance of Sailors and in extreme cases can result in a loss of security clearances and can drive vulnerable Sailors to poor financial and ethical decisions. While cases as extreme as this are relatively rare, a chain of command can expend considerable time and effort dealing with personal financial problems. When you become aware of a Sailor experiencing financial distress, the first thing to do is talk to the Sailor's chief, then inform your boss. How involved you and the chain of command become depends on the nature of the problem and the competence of the individual involved. Remember to use the CFS (and possibly counselors at the FFSC) to help the member. The local chapter of the Navy–Marine Corps Relief Society also offers budgeting assistance and no-interest loans for Sailors in financial difficulty: http://www.nmcrs.org.

Benefits

This section will briefly describe some of the benefits you are entitled to as a service member. Below you will find short descriptive paragraphs and Web addresses to get you pointed in the right direction if you wish to explore more.

Medical and Dental

As a service member, you have ready access to Navy-provided medical and dental care. This is relatively straightforward, but care for your dependents is a bit more complicated. Your dependents will obtain care through Tricare, the military's health management system. When enrolling in Tricare, your dependent will select one of the following three options for care as quoted from the Tricare Web site:

Tricare Prime is a managed care option similar to a civilian health maintenance organization (HMO). Active duty members and their families do not pay enrollment fees, annual deductibles, or co-payments for care in the TRICARE network.

Tricare Extra is a preferred provider option (PPO) in which beneficiaries choose a doctor, hospital, or other medical provider within the TRICARE provider network.

Tricare Standard is a fee-for-service option, meaning you can see an authorized Tricare provider of your choice. Having this flexibility means that care generally costs more.

For more information, see the Tricare Web site: https://www .tricareonline.com/tricareInfoCenter.do.

The Navy works to invest in its people and their families through pay, medical care, and a variety of other benefits. (U.S. Navy, JOSN Brandon Shelander)

Tricare also administers a dental insurance program for dependents, which covers limited dental work for a small monthly fee. More information is available here: http://www.tricare.mil/dental/default.cfm.

Life Insurance

When you join the Navy, you will be automatically enrolled into the Service Group Life Insurance (SGLI) program unless you specifically decline coverage. As of 2008, the preselected coverage is $400,000 for a monthly fee of $29 (which will automatically be deducted from your pay). Be sure that you update your "Page 2" at the admin office with the correct beneficiary information. The Department of Veterans Affairs (which administers SGLI) Web site has more information on SGLI, as well as other veteran's benefits: http://www.insurance.va.gov/sgliSite/SGLI/SGLI.htm.

Thrift Saving Plan

The Thrift Savings Plan (TSP) allows uniformed service members to contribute a certain percentage of their pay to a defined benefits retirement plan that offers many of the same tax and savings benefits of a civilian 401K. Briefly, you may contribute up to the annual limit ($15,000 in recent years) to a number of managed investment funds, deferring the tax on the contribution until withdrawal (presumably in retirement, when your income tax rate will be much lower). For further details, see the uniformed

service TSP Web site or talk to your command financial specialist: http://
www.tsp.gov/uniserv/features/chapter01.html.

Tuition Assistance
Most warfare communities desire their commissioned officers to obtain
a master's degree sometime after their initial tour. Options include the
Naval Postgraduate School, the Naval War College, an assortment of fel-
lowships, and various community specific programs such as the Surface
Warfare Officer Graduate Education Voucher. For specifics on these
programs, see the BUPERS graduate education Web site at http://www
.npc.navy.mil/Officer/Education_Placement/.

Many officers, however, choose to pursue advanced degrees on their
own time. Tuition assistance (TA) is available to offset the costs for continuing education at almost any accredited institution. As of 2008, TA pays
a maximum of $250 per semester hour, up to 16 semester hours per fiscal
year. Keep in mind that any officer who uses TA incurs a two-year service
obligation, which is served concurrently with any other obligation (in other
words, the obligation is not tacked on to the end of any other obligation
that you may have, but you will have to serve a minimum of two years from
the time you accept TA). For more on tuition assistance, visit the Navy
College TA site: https://www.navycollege.navy.mil/ta1.html.

Family Support Programs
The Fleet Family Support Center in your home port has a wide assortment
of programs available to help you and your family. These include:

★ Financial planning assistance. Classes and one-on-one counseling.
★ Relocation services. Help with planning your transfer.
★ New parent support. Education for new and soon-to-be parents.
★ Family employment. Assistance with résumé preparation, interview
skill building, and job searches for dependents.
★ Deployment support. Tips and support for families of service mem-
bers approaching and on deployment.

The FFSC also provides command support in cases involving domestic violence and sexual assault. The main FFSC Web site is located below,
but you should also search for the local FFSC in your home port: https://
www.nffsp.org/skins/nffsp/home.aspx.

VA Home Loan Benefit

Another benefit you should be aware of is the VA home loan guarantee. As a service member, you are entitled to a loan guarantee from the Veterans Administration that can help you get approved for a home loan and may significantly lower the interest rate you can obtain. For more information, visit the VA Home Loan site: http://www.homeloans.va.gov/index.htm.

Getting Financially Smart—for You and Your Sailors

The Navy's pay and benefit system can seem quite complex, but understanding your compensation will ensure that you are not incurring unnecessary expenses by paying for benefits that are already provided. More importantly, by understanding your compensation, you will be more prepared to help your Sailors should they have financial questions or encounter difficulties. Take some time to visit the Web sites listed in this chapter so you are comfortable with the terminology and your entitlements. Doing so will not only help you navigate your finances during your first years in the Navy, it will also profit the Sailors you lead.

★ 7 ★

UNDERSTANDING U.S. NAVY PROGRAMS AND POLICIES

As an organization strongly defined by its integrity and values, the U.S. Navy places a great deal of emphasis on the conduct, welfare, and employment of its people. Despite the sophisticated technology and tactics we employ, the Navy is a "people" business. As a newly commissioned officer, part of your role as a leader and manager of your Sailors will depend on your grasp of a wide variety of important programs and policies that support our Sailors. This chapter will provide some insight into the programs and policies that the U.S. Navy uses to help Sailors accomplish the mission.

While it is impossible to review every program or instruction that touches the lives of your Sailors, we will begin with the core values that guide our decision-making and management. Then we will move on to how leadership sets the course for our work. Finally, we will spend a large portion of the chapter looking at how the Navy helps us work together to support our families.

The U.S. Navy's Core Values

Honor, courage, commitment. These are the Navy's core values and they are the bedrock that forms the foundation of our service. As a newly commissioned officer, you are called to embody these characteristics and provide a role model for your Sailors to emulate. This is not an easy task because you will be making decisions under pressure, in a fast-moving environment, and with the potential to take men and women into harm's way. Even when you find yourself in an environment of relatively lower operational tempo and risk, your ethical decisions will signal to everyone around you how you can be counted on when there are tough decisions to be made.

To provide a more complete understanding of the Navy's interpretation of these fundamental building blocks, the Core Values Charter was developed and is maintained on the Internet homepages of the Navy and

The Navy is committed to creating an environment where every leader has the chance to excel and grow. (U.S. Navy, PHC Chris Desmond)

Marine Corps. The charter provides the following synopsis of the Navy's core values:

> *Honor.* I am accountable for my professional and personal behavior. I will be mindful of the privilege I have to serve my fellow Americans.
> *Courage.* Courage is the value that gives me the moral and mental strength to do what is right, with confidence and resolution, even in the face of temptation or adversity.
> *Commitment.* The day-to-day duty of every man and woman in the Department of the Navy is to join together as a team to improve the quality of our work, our people, and ourselves.

For many of your Sailors and fellow officers, these values naturally align with the ethical framework that they lived by prior to joining the Navy. For others, these values provide a departure from the life and difficulties they experienced prior to recruit training. Along with the senior enlisted who are your leadership partners, two of your roles as an officer are to ensure that your people are developing these values for themselves and to promote that growth. While describing how you build an ethical organizational climate is no easy task, you will never go wrong by setting the example in your personal conduct and signaling early that you will hold your team to the highest standards.

Understanding How and Why Naval Leaders Share Their Vision

After laying a general cultural foundation, one of the next tasks for leaders is to provide broad direction to their workforce on what the mission is and how it should be accomplished. Vision statements take many forms, and it is not always easy to grasp how broad servicewide concepts and policies translate to those "close to the deckplates." Although your Sailors will be learning the technical and tactical skills required to perform their roles, they will often look to you and your chief petty officer to connect what they are doing to the "big picture." Your success in this endeavor will depend on your taking the time to read, listen to, and eventually communicate broad naval policies and goals to the men and women who work for you.

Fortunately, our Navy's senior leadership has distilled broader policy into products that can be used by command leadership to share the Navy's mission, goals, and direction. Here are a few examples of policy documents and sources you may find useful:

★ *The New Maritime Strategy.* "A Cooperative Strategy for 21st Century Seapower" was presented by the Chief of Naval Operations (CNO) and the Commandants of the U.S. Marine Corps and U.S. Coast Guard at the International Seapower Symposium in Newport, Rhode Island, in October 2007. This strategy will apply maritime power to the critical protection of U.S. vital interests in an increasingly interconnected and uncertain world.

★ *Sea Power 21.* Published in 2002, *Sea Power 21* was ADM Vern Clark's overarching vision for the desired shape of the early-twenty-first-century Navy. It set a tone for the Navy to improve efficiency and set priorities for the future capabilities necessary to keep the Navy relevant and ready to meet the needs of the nation.

★ *The 1,000 Ship Navy.* This strategy paper published by the CNO's staff (frequently known as OPNAV) gives us general guidance on pursuing greater cooperation with our maritime partners around the world.

★ *Your Commanding Officer's Command Philosophy.* Most commanding officers will publish their intentions for the leadership and management of their command in a short document. This is an especially good way to get a feel for the leadership style of a new commanding officer.

★ *Naval Institute Proceedings.* This independent, professional journal is published monthly. It is often the first place to find major strategy papers from the CNO's staff. However, it is also a great resource to determine the role of your command in supporting a specific mission or theater of operations.

★ *The U.S. Navy Web Site.* This site, www.navy.mil, includes a multitude of policy guidance including the New Maritime Strategy, Sea Power 21, and the CNO's Annual Guidance to the Navy (also referred to as

"CNOG"—CNO's Guidance—and a good document to review every year). The Navy also features news updates, speeches from our Navy's leadership, and information sheets that will be immensely helpful to new officers looking to learn about the broader Navy.

Creating a Working Environment
Based on Mutual Support and Respect

The Navy has a number of programs in place to ensure that we enjoy a workplace that gives each one of us the chance to contribute to the mission and succeed without fear of discrimination or harassment. Human relationships are not always easily bound by written instructions, but your knowledge of these policies and commitment to the ideals behind these policies are essential to creating a command climate that allows all of your Sailors the chance to serve honorably.

Protecting Equal Opportunity, Preventing Sexual Harassment

Equal Opportunity (EO) is a program that ensures every member of a command has the opportunity to succeed without facing discrimination due to race, ethnicity, national origin, gender, or religion. The perception within a command that some Sailors are being discriminated against based on attributes beyond their control will be devastating to a command's morale and run counter to the Navy's core values. The instruction that guides our Navy's approach to Equal Opportunity is OPNAVINST 5354.1 series.

Every command is required to have a command-managed equal opportunity (CMEO) manager who is the single point of contact for EO issues and coordinates all complaint reports and resolutions. Should you ever be presented with a situation that is an EO violation or simply raises a question in your mind about EO, the CMEO manager is a person you should interact with at the first opportunity. Rest assured that your people will watch your reaction to a situation that is, or borders on, an EO violation. Like all standards, what you let pass without comment or action will become the new level of acceptable behavior, so be vigilant in your efforts to address equal opportunity violations and concerns.

Both the EO policy and sexual harassment policy (SECNAVINST 5300.26C) provide guidance to prevent and stop sexual harassment. They broadly define what behavior is acceptable, borderline, and unacceptable using a stoplight scale (green, yellow, and red light behavior). These same instructions delineate the process for reporting and addressing EO and sexual harassment issues. The instructions utilize a "reasonable person" standard to determine if sexual harassment has occurred, but recognizing the human dimension involved in this approach, you should avoid conversations, e-mails, or content of a sexual nature, just as you would in most civilian work environments.

The key to dealing with reports of sexual harassment is to deal with them honestly, quickly, and in accordance with the Navy's policies. Like many problems you will face in the Navy and in life, failing to respond promptly and properly to sexual harassment will almost always make the problem worse. Sexual harassment issues should be handled at the lowest appropriate level based on the specifics of the individual case.

Based on the severity of the issue or inability to resolve it, the CMEO manager should be informed for formal action. Sexual harassment is damaging to good order, discipline, and morale within a command. As a leader, you play a significant role in setting the proper example and taking quick action on violations of the Navy's EO and sexual harassment guidance.

Sexual Assault Victim Intervention (SAVI) Program

Sexual assault is a criminal act and runs counter to the Navy's core values. Whether the assault occurs at work or at home, with a shipmate or otherwise, the event will have a traumatic impact in any victim's life, both personally and professionally. As a result, the Navy created the SAVI program to establish a codified process for dealing with these very sensitive situations.

The OPNAVINST 1752.1 series provides the details of this program and defines sexual assault as "intentional sexual contact, characterized by use of force, physical threat or abuse of authority or when the victim does not or cannot consent. Sexual assault includes rape, nonconsensual sodomy, indecent assault, or attempts to commit these acts. Sexual assault can occur without regard to gender." An important distinction is that sexual assault and sexual harassment are two completely different offenses, and the response to each is governed by different instructions. Again, sexual assault involves the use of force and is a crime under the Uniform Code of Military Justice.

To support and care for the victim, each command is required to have SAVI representatives who act as an initial support structure for the victim. As a leader, it is important to ensure that any Sailor who needs to speak with a SAVI representative is afforded an opportunity without delay. With the vast majority of the Navy operating in a mixed gender work environment, it is important to know who your command's SAVI representative is and to ensure that you and the team you lead are receiving periodic SAVI training.

Fraternization

Fraternization is the term traditionally used to identify personal relationships which contravene the customary bounds of acceptable senior–subordinate relationships.

OPNAVINST 5370.2 SERIES.

Although fraternization is often characterized as a male–female issue, any unduly familiar relationship that fails to respect differences in rank and authority constitutes a violation even if both people are the same gender. Relationships of a personal nature between officers and enlisted, and senior enlisted (E-7 and above) and junior enlisted (E-6 and below) are prohibited. However, the Navy's policies do allow for inclusive participation in command-sponsored events such as picnics and membership on sports teams.

Relationships that constitute fraternization are prejudicial to good order and discipline and are another danger to the unity and efficiency of a command. Like other policies designed to manage human behavior, the exact point at which a relationship becomes unduly familiar may be difficult to identify, so you will again want to be particularly vigilant to not let a professional relationship lapse into a personal one. Keep relationships with your subordinates completely professional and take tactful but decisive action in correcting a subordinate who attempts to draw you toward the gray area of this policy. While you must vigilantly live by the Navy's fraternization policy, do not let a distorted fear of regulations completely isolate you from your Sailors. Common sense and a positive but professional tone with your Sailors will keep you on the right track.

Supporting Navy Families

It takes a great deal of dedication to maintain the world's finest Navy, and our families play an important role in this effort. Accordingly, the Navy's senior leadership has developed programs and policies to assist families in working through the challenges military families face.

The best resource for leaders to turn to for guidance in this area is the local Fleet and Family Support Center (FFSC). FFSC provides valuable support to the fleet by providing counsel to Sailors on subjects ranging from parenting skills to marriage counseling and financial management. They are especially helpful to families with both spouses in the military. These counselors provide direct support to families, and they train senior Sailors and officers to provide counsel to shipmates when direct support from shore facilities is not available.

FFSC also provides training to another key family resource, command ombudsmen. The command ombudsman is the spouse of a member of the command who volunteers to serve as the link between the families and the command. The ombudsman is appointed by the commanding officer and serves the command by listening to the concerns of Sailors' families, keeping them informed on certain aspects of the ship's schedule and operations, and connecting those families with challenges to those support structures that can provide help. Just as important, the ombudsman plays a vital role in assisting the commanding officer and command master chief in their efforts to be responsive to the family readiness of their command.

Family Advocacy Program

Just as with sexual abuse, the abuse of a child or spouse is never excusable and is inconsistent with the Navy's core values. The Family Advocacy Program (FAP) provides clinical assessment, treatment, and services for military members and their families involved in incidents of domestic abuse in order to protect victims from future abuse. The guiding instruction on the FAP, SECNAVINST 1752.3B, lists five primary goals for this program:

★ Prevention
★ Victim safety and protection
★ Offender accountability
★ Rehabilitative education and counseling
★ Community accountability/responsibility for a consistent appropriate response

FAP is a command program and leadership effort that focuses on reducing incidents of child and domestic abuse and getting treatment and care for victims. If you encounter the possibility of child abuse within a Navy family, be sure to contact your chain of command and the command's family advocacy representative right away—the unacceptability of child and domestic abuse as well the related legal and privacy issues warrant an immediate but well-informed response from you and your command.

Personal Readiness

The Navy takes a great deal of interest in the well-being of Sailors in all facets of life. While in service to the nation, we enjoy complete medical care and the considerable benefits of commissaries and the Navy Exchange. We also are supported by a wide variety of programs that ensure we are healthy and productive citizens and family members.

Physical Readiness

Physical fitness is a crucial element of mission performance and must be a part of every Sailor's life. Mission readiness and operational effectiveness are built on the physical fitness of the individual; therefore, all naval personnel shall maintain personal physical fitness by regular exercise and proper nutrition.

OPNAVINST 6110.1H

In the last two decades, many business sectors have concluded that healthy workers are generally happier, healthier, and more productive in society, and the Navy is no exception. Just as important, many of the missions our Sailors will perform, particularly those in an operational or crisis environment, require every U.S. Navy service member to be fit. Unfortunately, you may encounter otherwise very effective Sailors who jeopardize their career due to an inability to maintain required physical readiness and body fat standards. Make every effort you can to support your Sailors in improving their fitness and ensure that those who struggle to maintain the standards are working closely with the command fitness leader (CFL) to improve their physical condition.

The physical fitness assessment (PFA) must be completed on a semiannual basis. The test consists of four basic parts: body fat evaluation, flexibility, aerobic capacity, and muscular strength. Body fat is first evaluated under a "go, no-go" test based only on a member's height and weight. If members are over the prescribed weight (see OPNAVINST 6110.1H), they are measured in several places on their bodies with a measuring tape. These measurements are then used to determine a body fat percentage.

The last three portions of the PFA are completed by demonstrating flexibility in the "sit and reach" test; muscular strength in the push up and sit up test; and cardiovascular condition in the 1.5 mile run or 500 yard swim. Treadmill, elliptical, and exercise bicycle tests are also now available as well.

Sailors who fail to meet minimum standards are required to participate in their command's fitness enhancement program to ensure they have an opportunity to improve their physical condition under a structured workout regimen. Any Sailor who fails three or more tests in a four-year span becomes eligible for administrative separation from the Navy.

Alcohol and Drug Use

Drug and alcohol abuse pose a severe threat to a Sailor's combat readiness in terms of performance, reliability, judgment, and time lost. It undermines health, safety, discipline, and loyalty. Drug and alcohol abuse is incompatible with the maintenance of high standards of performance, military discipline, and readiness and is destructive of U.S. Navy efforts to instill pride, promote professionalism, and enhance personal excellence.

OPNAVINST 5350.4C

At your duty station, the drug and alcohol prevention advisor (DAPA) is tasked with assisting the commanding officer in ensuring the requirements of the Navy's drug and alcohol abuse prevention and control policy

(OPNAVINST 5350.4C) are followed. The basic tenets of the policy are zero tolerance for drug use and responsible use of alcohol for those of legal age. Any Sailor who is caught or who admits to using illegal drugs of any kind must be processed for separation from the Navy by his or her commanding officer.

The alcohol use policy issues clear guidelines with respect to Sailors who commit "alcohol related incidents" (ARI). An ARI is any violation of the Uniform Code of Military Justice (UCMJ), including public drunkenness and driving under the influence, committed where, in the judgment of the CO, alcohol was a contributing factor. If the violation is severe, the Sailor is administratively discharged. If the violation is less severe, the Sailor will be directed to attend alcohol abuse treatment coordinated by the DAPA. Should a Sailor have any additional ARIs, he or she would be administratively discharged.

The days of "drinking like a Sailor" and irresponsible behavior while on liberty are over. Commands are directed to deglamorize the use of alcohol and apply measures to ensure all hands are trained on the professional and physical effects of alcohol use and abuse. Command-sponsored events must provide a nonalcoholic beverage option and must strictly prohibit any participation in activities that encourage excessive and irresponsible drinking.

For anyone, including yourself, who has an alcohol-dependence problem, the best solution is reaching out for help to the DAPA before any disciplinary action is initiated. This approach is called self-referral; it enables the DAPA to provide the needed treatment without the negative consequences associated with alcohol related incidents. For instance, it is not appropriate for evaluators to reference a self-referral in any way on a Sailor's evaluation.

Alcohol use is another area where your on-duty and off-duty example will support and encourage Sailors to do the same. When junior officers put themselves in a situation where their Sailors, or their superiors, observe them abusing alcohol, they undermine their effectiveness as leaders. Unfortunately, alcohol is often a contributing factor in many of the other issues addressed in this chapter including fraternization, sexual harassment, and sexual assault.

Voting Assistance

The U.S. Navy voting assistance program is in place to ensure eligible naval personnel have an opportunity to vote in federal, state, and local elections. Your command's voting assistance officer will provide all the required materials necessary to register to vote for all elections requested by Sailors at their commands. The key goal is to provide every Sailor the opportunity to vote; it is not a mandatory voting program and should obviously stay apolitical in approach. A good voting assistance program will reinforce commitment to our democratic principles and encourage a citizen's individual responsibility to participate in government.

Volunteer Programs and Charitable Causes

The Navy also recognizes the importance of encouraging Sailors to engage their communities both at home and while deployed. Every command should have a volunteer programs coordinator who plans and organizes community relations (COMREL) projects. These projects can be simple Saturday morning events such as cleanups at local beaches, but they can also have far-reaching effects, such as building a playground for disadvantaged schoolchildren during a foreign port visit. Large commands in your area and embassy staffs in foreign countries can help you find great opportunities to make a difference in the community if you join your command's volunteer program.

Another way to get involved in your community is to support charitable causes. The Combined Federal Campaign (CFC) is a federal government–wide program that provides a listing of thousands of legitimate and reputable charitable causes and enables federal employees to make donations through regular deductions from your paycheck. CFC conducts a fund drive every year, and each command has a coordinator who ensures that everyone has the opportunity to support the cause of his or her choice. Additionally, the Navy–Marine Corps Relief Society, an organization dedicated to supporting our Sailors and their families in need, holds an annual fund drive separate from the Combined Federal Campaign.

Understanding Our Values, Taking Care of Our Sailors, Accomplishing the Mission

The U.S. Navy is a successful yet complex organization that focuses on "mission first, and Sailors always." From our fundamental values to our families and to the physical, mental, and professional well-being of every Sailor, the Navy has programs and policies to support the mission and the individual Sailor. As a new officer, you must strive to be aware of the programs and policies so you can support your command—and your Sailors—to the very best of your abilities.

★ 8 ★

NAVAL CORRESPONDENCE AND ADMINISTRATION

W hile administrative management is not the first thing that comes to mind when we think about the naval profession, the reality is that this is an important competency in the modern Navy. Treating administrative duties with contempt or merely as an afterthought will not serve you well. More importantly, if an officer neglects administrative duties, his Sailors will be the real losers. Reenlistment forms, command awards, evaluations, and applications for hazardous duty pay are all "paperwork" that will be deeply important to the Sailors who serve with you.

In addition to the paperwork affiliated with your Sailors' quality of life and personal advancement, you will encounter administrative requirements that intersect every aspect of naval life (mission, safety, personnel, finance). Just as importantly, although mission accomplishment and results matter most, one of the ways you will build your reputation at your first command will be based on the quality of the work you do, and your very first responsibilities will very likely be administrative in nature.

As you gain experience, you will start to identify what projects demand near perfection and which ones are more perfunctory in nature, but always be mindful that every product you approve or sign off helps to establish your standards. If your immediate boss has questions about a product that comes from your division or organization, he will not be interested in talking to whoever wrote the first draft; he will want to talk to you, so make sure you have command of the details in the document.

The Goal: "All But the Signature" Staffwork

As you work on the myriad of administrative requirements that face a newly commissioned officer, you may wonder what the goal or purpose of each item or requirement is. Although these are legitimate questions, you should view your efforts through a broader prism. Simply put, your goal should be that your boss could approve every document you have prepared without any amendments. Realistically, your boss' experience and finer eye will likely result in changes that improve the document, but if you give every product your best, you will certainly be much more successful in your administrative endeavors.

As you drive toward the goal of complete staffwork, remember to ensure that your input is indeed complete. If your administrative package requires a cover memo or endorsement from your chain of command, for example, draft them for inclusion. As you will be encouraged to do elsewhere in this book, ask yourself, "What would I want if I were the boss?" and you will be on your way to meeting the "all but the signature" standard.

Timeliness

Although the notion that paperwork and correspondence should be on time seems obvious, it bears emphasis because most junior officers (and senior ones for that matter) will have to work very hard to meet deadlines. Life at a naval command is busy and rightfully focused on primary mission accomplishment. That notwithstanding, you will be expected to meet administrative deadlines as well as operational ones.

The good news is that you can plan for the majority of administrative work tasks you will face. Evaluations, end-of-tour awards, and end-of-year items such as command histories are all scheduled requirements for which you can plan. Most successful commands maintain an "admin tickler" to track these requirements; you should apply this concept to your own administrative requirements by maintaining your own admin tickler cataloging all the scheduled reports, evaluations, and products that you will be expected to generate. By managing these well, you will be better prepared for the pop-up requirements that are a fact of life in the fast-paced environment you will live in as a newly commissioned officer.

Write Clearly

If you have recently emerged from a collegiate environment, the style of writing you will use in a naval setting will almost certainly be different than what you used in an academic setting. Good naval writing is much closer to a newspaper style vice that of a longer book or term paper and is clear, concise, and to the point. Unlike some academic writing, where sentence after sentence is dedicated to buttress each point, most naval writing requires you to get your facts in order, get to the main point quickly, and complete the tasking in no more than a page or two. As officers become more senior and face larger numbers of increasingly complex issues, the demand for clear, concise writing only increases.

An ensign prepares an intelligence brief while deployed. (U.S. Navy, MC3 Patrick Gearhiser)

In addition to keeping things short, there are other tips that will serve you well in your writing. Avoid overusing all but the most commonly understood acronyms. If you need to use acronyms that will not be obvious to everyone who will read your work, use the full term first followed by the acronym in parentheses—for example, Aegis Training and Readiness Center (ATRC)—and then use the acronym thereafter to save space.

Avoid using overly stiff language and the passive voice. It is perfectly fine to use plain language such as "Next time, we need to pay attention to current and wind" vice "Wind and current must be accounted for in the future and for all additional evolutions." Additionally, avoid using filler words that are unnecessary to the meaning of a sentence, such as "in the future" or "at this time."

Finally, make sure that you carefully proofread any document you are passing up the chain of command, and consider asking another peer to proofread any work that you primarily drafted to provide a second set of eyes on the document. Since most administration you complete will be one or two pages in length, consider reading the document aloud to see if it is easy to understand. Remember, your goal is not to have the reader marvel at your writing style but to help your seniors quickly assess the facts and make a decision.

Avoid Reinventing the Wheel

Since most naval administration is repetitive in nature (evaluations, supply orders, collateral duty designations, for example), locate a previous example to guide your efforts. Although doing this will not guarantee success, reviewing the last version—particularly a final, approved version that has "been sent off the command"—will demonstrate what the command standard has been previously.

In many cases, administrative requirements are so repetitive that your predecessor may have prepared templates to guide preparation. No one will expect you to have these formats memorized, but you will be expected to have reviewed this information beforehand. If your predecessor has not turned over a file (or thumb drive) of common administrative products associated with your duties, you should start to build your own for future reference. Your naval peers and your administrative office will also be good sources for identifying successful administrative examples for you to emulate.

What's the Reference?

Even if you have the previous example of an administrative requirement, you will want to review the actual reference that guides the program or product you are working on. If this is the first time you are responsible for the document, your boss will almost certainly ask you if you have reviewed the reference. Additionally, no individual or command is perfect, so it is worth ensuring that the example your predecessor used is correct. Finally, naval references are routinely updated and streamlined, so a quick review of the reference will ensure that you are not using an out-of-date instruction. Your administrative officer will have a catalog of all naval instructions for you to use and reference, but you should build your own reference library to support your most common administrative products.

The Point Paper

The U.S. Navy Correspondence Manual provides you guidance on writing naval memos and letters, but one of the most common products you will be required to produce is a "point paper." This is usually a one-page, streamlined memo that highlights a given issue, outlines several options to address it, and makes a recommendation (make sure to ask for an example of a point or issue paper at your new command).

If you bring up a dilemma or new challenge to your boss, you may hear him or her ask that you "work up a point paper on the issue." Over time, if you encounter an issue or challenge that you want to share with your boss on your own initiative, you may find yourself composing a point paper to share this challenge with your chain of command. Although every command or staff will likely follow a slightly different format for this document, the point paper is a weapon you will want to have in your "administrative arsenal."

E-mail

Just as e-mail has impacted business and society in general, it has also permeated almost every aspect of naval life over the last fifteen years. For young officers, communicating via e-mail has become second nature—often preferred to talking on the phone because of its convenience and ability to save time in communicating. E-mail communications are certainly a staple of naval business and communications, and e-mail has enabled naval personnel to much more easily communicate both within and outside the lifelines of their commands.

Your comfort with e-mail in your personal and academic life, however, should not lull you into a false sense of complacency when it comes to e-mail in your workplace in the Navy. As you have likely discovered elsewhere, e-mail can be forwarded quite easily, much more so than phone conversations or hard copy communications, and any ill-considered comment in e-mail has the ability to bounce around the information superhighway in a far more lasting way than a verbal remark.

Despite the potential pitfalls, using e-mail in the Navy is a necessary skill set and one that can save you work and time if you use it appropriately. If the e-mail is sent to a senior, make sure that it begins by addressing your senior by name ("Commander Jones") or at the very least with "Sir" or "Ma'am." Be sure to finish with the appropriate closing ("Very respectfully" or "V/r"). Remembering these tips will keep you from having an otherwise solid e-mail not get the reception it deserves.

If an idea is overly complex or takes more than a screen of text to explain, consider another communication format. If you find yourself writing a multiple page e-mail, a written memo, naval message, or perhaps an old-fashioned personal conversation may be a better option to convey your points. Recognize that in most quarters of the Navy, e-mail is still not perceived to be as permanent or "official" as a written naval message. A good general rule is to respond to whatever tasking you receive via the same forum—answer a naval message with a message, e-mail with e-mail, and so on.

While it is a good practice in general to avoid "transmitting" any message in anger, regardless of the forum, the permanent nature and ease with which e-mail can be forwarded warrants additional thought before you press "send." You are expected to give honest feedback and assessments;

nevertheless, recognize that anything negative you include in an e-mail could be forwarded on to the person or command you may be criticizing. Once again, give some thought as to whether e-mail is the best forum for the message you want to convey.

Be careful not to convey sensitive or classified information on unclassified e-mail systems. The handling of classified material will be covered later in this chapter, but it is important to state here that because of the ease with which information can be transmitted via e-mail, you should be very careful to make sure the information you send is appropriately classified.

Remember that e-mail "business rules" may vary from command to command. In some commands, it may be preferred for you to provide your boss with a simple status update via e-mail while in others your boss may expect a face-to-face update. Check with your peers or a more experienced junior officer to find out what works at your command.

Finally, if you have bad news to pass to your boss, do not take the easy way out by sending an e-mail to avoid a tough conversation. Being a naval officer requires fortitude, and part of the job requires that you can deliver the tough news truthfully. If you are compelled to deliver bad news via e-mail due to distance or other operational constraints, be sure to take responsibility for the problem, not make excuses, and provide the way ahead to a solution.

Counseling, Discipline, and Performance

Some of the most common—and important—administrative work you will do will be related to the performance assessment of your people. The instruction that governs the Navy's performance evaluation system (BUPERSINST 1610.10A) is accessible on the Internet and is the principal reference for performance evaluation in the Navy. Many officers print out the most recent version of this instruction to include as a part of their desk references because writing fitness reports and evaluations is a constant requirement in the Navy.

This guide will tell you when performance evaluations and formal counseling are required and how they should be prepared; this is worth periodically reviewing. Successful commands will be tracking performance evaluations at the command level, but you should know the required reporting periods and work ahead so your work is not diminished because you are rushing to meet an unanticipated deadline.

In addition to these formal requirements, you may be compelled to develop counseling sheets for Sailors who are not meeting standards in performance, physical fitness, and so on. While most Sailors are superb professionals, you will occasionally encounter Sailors who have fallen short in an aspect of their professional development. Documenting these deficiencies is critical, so be sure to touch base with your command's senior enlisted advisor and your department head to determine what format you should use when administering written counseling. Generally this type of counseling should document the problem, identify deficiencies, provide guidance, and include a future date where the individual's performance is reappraised.

If one of your Sailors ever commits an alleged violation of the UCMJ, he may wind up standing before the Executive Officer Inquiry (XOI) or Captain's Mast for punishment. Your command's legal officer will be able to assist your Sailor with the case and answer any questions you may have. Over time (and generally after other leadership steps have failed) you may be compelled to draft a "report chit" against one of your Sailors who has violated an article of the UCMJ. As in all cases where the UCMJ may be involved, seek out the advice of your department head and your command's legal officer to ensure that you are executing your legal and leadership responsibilities appropriately.

While the topic of nonjudicial punishment (NJP) is an important one, it is not covered here in depth. Recognize, however, that as your Sailors make their way through the administration of the system, you will be expected to support them and assist them with their needs. This does not mean that you will be required to defend their conduct or serve as their "lawyer," but you will need to work with your legal officer to ensure your Sailors are receiving the time and services they need.

In many of these proceedings, you, as the division officer (and likely your chief as well), will be required to provide a brief assessment or overview of the service member's performance to the CO or XO. Be prepared to provide this assessment and be ready to field questions related to previous actions you have taken, such as formal counseling. Commanding officers dislike disciplinary proceedings as much as you do, and most administer NJP as a last resort. As they administer punishment, they will be very interested in the leadership and professional climate that the affected Sailor works in. Making sure that you have your "i"s dotted and "t"s crossed will assist the CO in his assessment of the case and prevent you from not being prepared.

Personal and Command Awards

You will also play a role in preparing awards for your Sailors. If you have not come from a military background, it is difficult to overstate how important this recognition is to Sailors—even if they say otherwise. With bonuses and other incentives largely controlled on a broad Navy-wide basis, awards serve as one of the primary vehicles naval leaders use to recognize and reward strong performance at the command level. While getting your Sailors recognized will likely be a very satisfying process, managing and administering the awards process requires effort.

The practice of using a reference to find previously successful examples to guide your administrative efforts pertains to awards management and generation as well. In this case you should seek out the awards manual for your chain of command (most carrier and expeditionary strike groups, for example, have issued their own instructions) and review previously successful examples and templates used by your command.

Awards are generally comprised of three elements: the citation, an awards form, and a longer justification that details achievements that demonstrate why the nominee is deserving of the award. As your experience grows and you have a chance to see an award progress from your first draft to an actual medal awarded to one of your Sailors, make an effort to get a look at the final approved product. By closely comparing it to your original effort you can identify the items you will want to improve the next time.

Just as in other cases, planning ahead of the game will help you do your best by your people. You may occasionally have the opportunity to write an "impact award" honoring a specific and unexpected act of excellence by one of your Sailors, but the vast majority of awards can be anticipated because most occur at the end of deployments, the end of the training cycle of an operational command, or the end of an individual service member's tour. In many cases commands reward the majority of Sailors completing their tour with a personal medal—so be ready to dedicate a significant level of effort to this area.

By leaning forward and generating first drafts of their awards packages for your deserving Sailors, you are on your way to representing them well. Enterprising young officers have been able to create opportunities for recognition by having things prepared when their bosses inevitably ask, "Who do we want to recognize for this event?" As you advocate for your Sailors, your peers will be fighting hard for their Sailors as well. Maturely recognize that you may not be able to award a medal to every person you deem deserving. If this is the case, look for other ways to recognize good performance, such as a letter of commendation and a letter of appreciation.

In addition to awards for your Sailors, you may also play a role in preparing year-end awards for your command. Most commands compete for the Battle Efficiency Award as well as the subordinate mission excellence awards related to maintenance, safety, and warfare effectiveness. These awards usually require commands to create narratives of their achievements as well as meet certain performance milestones. To be ready for this, consider keeping a list of achievements over the course of the year so you are not starting from scratch in the eleventh month of a twelve-month competitive cycle.

References

As you prepare to win the "admin battle," consider building a small professional library to help you in this endeavor. You will find a number of the references below in your command spaces, but you may want to consider purchasing some of these after you have had a chance to review a peer's copy. For naval references included in the list below, if you do not want to print out a paper copy, consider downloading a copy to the hard drive of your computer.

★ Dictionary
★ *Division Officer's Guide* (RADM James G. Stavridis and CDR Robert Girrier, Naval Institute Press, 2004)
★ Navy Correspondence Manual
★ Navy Performance Evaluation Instruction
★ Awards Manual
★ Recurring reports tickler
★ File of previously successful reports and administrative products

Working with Classified Material

One element of your profession that separates you from the vast majority of your civilian peers is that you will likely work with classified material. Classified material is any information that, if disclosed to unauthorized people, could jeopardize U.S. interests, institutions, foreign relations, or national security. Three classification levels exist:

★ Top Secret: Information the unauthorized disclosure of which reasonably could be expected to cause exceptionally grave damage to the national security.
★ Secret: Information the unauthorized disclosure of which reasonably could be expected to cause serious damage to the national security.
★ Confidential: Information the unauthorized disclosure of which reasonably could be expected to cause damage to the national security.

Given the critical nature of classified information, there are very clear directives in place to guide its use. As long as you have access to classified material, you will receive periodic security awareness briefings. Each command will have a security officer who will arrange these briefs to remind you of your responsibilities to communicate security changes that affect you. As a condition of continued access to this information, you have an obligation to report any changes in your personal status to your security officer. Some of these changes include:

★ Attempts by unauthorized individuals to obtain classified or proprietary information
★ Loss or possible compromise of classified information
★ Any major financial difficulties
★ Violations of the law or arrests
★ Alcoholism or treatment of alcoholism or illegal use of drugs
★ Involvement in court or legal proceedings

If you are working with classified material, you are normally required to work in a secure area. During the workday, secure areas are protected with a combination of access control systems, security, and identification badges. After hours, locks, alarms, and motion detectors are activated to prevent unauthorized access.

Need to Know

When sharing classified information with co-workers, you must be sure that they have not only the appropriate clearances and access levels but also a clear "need-to-know." Establishing "need to know" is important in controlling classified material. To make this determination, whoever holds classified material should ask w*hy does the other person need the information?* If you have doubts about the person's need to know, you should either politely deny the person access or state that you need to seek additional guidance before providing access. Contact your security officer for advice.

Discussing Classified Information

To discuss classified program information, you must use a secure area that has been specifically accredited for the particular programs to which you have access. Be aware that common passageways, bathrooms, dining areas, gyms, garages, commercial airlines, vehicles, and so on are not approved areas for classified discussions. When discussing classified material, you may use only secure communications. Secure telephone systems operate in a continuous secure mode with other telephones in the system. STU-III telephones, conversely, are secure only when they have been switched to secure voice mode.

The explosion of personal electronic devices has also affected how we handle classified material. In most commands, personal electronic devices (telephones, pagers, or BlackBerries) either are not allowed in a space that is cleared for classified information or are turned off. Some of these facilities will further require that your BlackBerry be turned off and batteries removed from your cell phone while you are in the cleared space or facility.

Doing Your Best in All Things

It is doubtful that any of our modern-day naval leaders and heroes have ever aspired to be known as the "Great Administrator." Nevertheless, naval correspondence and administration will likely play a significant role in your duties and responsibilities. Being a mature leader means doing the things you like to do least to the best of your abilities, and if you approach these responsibilities in this spirit, your command, your Sailors, and you will benefit in the long run.

★ 9 ★

MANAGING YOUR CAREER

lthough the Navy values teamwork above all, this is a competitive profession, and you will ultimately be measured against
a large number of other highly competent officers when your
record comes before a promotion or screening board. The Navy's personnel selection system is regarded as highly fair; nevertheless, for you to
reach your next career milestone, understanding what the Navy requires
is essential.

Promotion and Screening Boards

The Bureau of Naval Personnel (BUPERS) uses a board review process to competitively select the best officers for promotion, and to screen
candidates for various career milestones such as eligibility for command at
sea. Promotion boards are termed "statutory" in that the number of officers that can be selected to each grade is dictated by Congress. Screening
boards (also known as administrative boards) are largely governed by the
Navy and the service community itself and are focused on selecting officers for further responsibilities within their community such as department head or command.

★ BUPERS promotion board page: http://www.npc.navy.mil/Boards/
GeneralBoardInfo/
★ BUPERS screening board page: http://www.npc.navy.mil/Boards/
ScreenBoards/

The Detailer

The detailer is your direct representative at BUPERS. He or she "details"
officers into specific jobs, balancing desires, career requirements, and the
needs of the Navy. When you reach approximately nine months from your
planned rotation date (PRD) from your current command, you will begin
a dialog with the detailer that concludes with orders for your next tour.

As a starting point, the list of available jobs is published on the BUPERS Web site for your particular community.

When your career, personal, and naval needs align, this process can be relatively easy. On occasion, however, you may have to do a job that is not at the top of your preferences. As you work through this process, remember that the detailer is an officer from your own community who can be a valuable career counselor—he or she sees hundreds of records from your community. If you are detailed to a job that is not your first choice, "bloom where you are planted"—your strong performance in a tough job will almost always be rewarded over the long run.

Unrestricted and Restricted Line
Unrestricted line officers (often referred to as "URL," or "line officers") form the leadership of the Navy and its three traditional warfare communities: surface, subsurface, or aviation. They operate and command surface ships, submarines, aircraft, and the majority of shore installations. There are a good number of subcommunities within the line category, including engineering duty officers and special duty officers in public affairs, foreign area, and oceanography. These officers are largely drawn from the three major line communities after earning their warfare designation via a lateral transfer selection board process.

Staff corps officers (otherwise known as "restricted line") have more narrowly focused, yet no less vital, responsibilities in support of commanders and the line communities. Unlike special duty assignment line officers, staff corps officers are initially commissioned into their fields. Often these specialists, such as supply officers and medical service corps officers, will primarily work within one of the primary warfare communities. Each staff corps has a unique insignia worn on the right collar in place of the normal rank insignia (line officers wear rank insignia on both collars).

Typical Career Paths
All officers follow different career paths to success, but it is possible to lay out what a notional career might look like for each officer community.

Surface Warfare Officer
Surface warfare officers (SWO) operate, maintain, and "drive" surface warships that continuously operate around the world. As a SWO, you can expect alternating assignments between sea duty on an operational warship and duty ashore on a staff, in a program office, or in a training facility. The typical SWO career path is laid out in the Career Planner on the PERS-41

As you progress in the Navy, strong operational performance will factor prominently in your selection for future leadership responsibilities. (U.S. Navy, MC2 Joseph R. Vincent)

Web site: http://www.npc.navy.mil/Officer/SurfaceWarfare/Career+Info/ SWOCareerPlanner.htm.

As a new SWO, you can expect to do two division officer tours at sea soon after commissioning. During your first tour you will pursue numerous qualifications, culminating in earning your surface warfare officer pin. Your first two tours will together total approximately four years. Each individual tour length depends on which division officer sequencing plan (DOSP) you elect (some officers will "fleet up" to a different job on the same ship, for instance, while others will go to a second tour job that requires a significant amount of schooling en route).

Following your division officer tours, you will go ashore for roughly three years. Most officers obtain a postgraduate degree during this period using one of the Navy's educational programs or on their own time while at another shore billet. Following your shore tour and department head training in Newport, Rhode Island, you will serve as a department head, responsible for a major functional area on your next ship (usually operations, engineering, or weapons). Normal command tours begin at roughly fifteen years of commissioned service (you will serve fifteen months as the XO, then fifteen months as the CO), although there are also earlier command opportunities available for exceptional officers. For more information on both conventional and the surface nuclear pipeline, visit the PERS-41 Web site: http://www.npc.navy.mil/Officer/SurfaceWarfare/.

Aviation

Aviation career paths are deeply affected by the particular community (e.g., F-18 Hornet, SH-60B Seahawk) that an officer is assigned to, but communities share some general traits. Student naval aviators (SNA) initially report to Pensacola, Florida, for the beginning of up to two years of training. While in Pensacola, SNAs undergo aviation preflight indoctrination (API) and primary flight training, then are selected for one of four paths: multiengine prop, helicopter, tail-hook (carrier aircraft), or EA-6B Prowler. Intermediate and advanced flight training follows at various locations around the United States.

Upon completion of advanced training, aviators are "winged" and report to one of the fleet replacement squadrons for training in a particular airframe. Fully qualified aviators are then assigned to an operational squadron for their first sea tour. This path is essentially the same for pilots and naval flight officers (NFO), with the exception that advanced training will be in weapons system operation vice flying for NFOs.

A shore tour can follow after three years in an operational squadron, often as a flight instructor or assigned to a staff. The next operational tour is normally a "disassociated" tour on an afloat staff or as ship's company on an aircraft carrier, perhaps as assistant navigator or the "shooter" operating the ship's catapults. If screened for department head, most officers will leave their disassociated tour after two years for fleet replacement squadron retraining and a job as a squadron department head for roughly three years. Following post–department head shore tour, screened officers report to a squadron as XO, then "fleet up" to be CO after approximately eighteen months. The PERS-43 Web site contains additional information: http://www.npc.navy.mil/Officer/Aviation/.

Submarine Officer

Submarine officers operate and maintain the Navy's nuclear submarines. All submarine officers are nuclear-power qualified, which involves well over a year of formal academic training before reporting to your first boat. After acceptance into the nuclear pipeline, an officer will report to Naval Nuclear Power Training Command in Charleston, South Carolina, for twenty-four weeks of intensive classroom training. After graduating, you will report to one of the prototype shore-based reactors for six months of further training. At the completion of the training pipeline, the next stop is ten weeks at the Submarine School in New London, Connecticut, for the Submarine Officer Basic Course (SOBC).

Division officers can expect to spend thirty-two months on their first boat, qualifying in submarines (earning your gold dolphins) and serving as engineer officer. Two years of shore duty follow the first sea tour, during which many officers will earn a master's degree. Officers next undergo the seven-month Submarine Officer Advance Course in New London and then report to their next submarine as a department head for thirty-two months. Successive shore and sea tours include a twenty-month XO tour at the twelve-year point with command occurring at the sixteen-year point. The submarine officer career path can be found at the PERS-42 submarine Web site: http://www.npc.navy.mil/Officer/SubmarineNuclear/.

Special Warfare Officer

Special warfare officers comprise a very small but incredibly capable and revered portion of the Navy's officer inventory. Officers join the community through both initial accession commissioning and lateral transfer. These warriors have proven their worth throughout the global war on terror, and more senior special warfare officers are rising to senior command and flag ranks. The Web sites below include excellent resources for new or aspiring special warfare officers:

★ BUPERS SPECWAR site: http://www.npc.navy.mil/OfficerSPECWAR/
★ Navy SEAL site: http://www.seal.navy.mil/
★ Career path: http://www.npc.navy.mil/NR/rdonlyres/AF686BFE-E7B0
-4A0E-94F4-D278B4E8AD7C/0/NSWOfficerCareerpath.ppt (password required for entry to site)

Special Duty Assignment Officers

As discussed above, these officers are specialists within the line community, selected by a lateral transfer/redesignation board (one notable exception is the intelligence community, which does accept some newly commissioned officers). The competitive semiannual transfer/redesignation board selects the best-qualified officers for each community after taking into consideration both the needs of the gaining community and the candidate's existing community. Each type of special duty assignment is briefly discussed below.

Engineering Duty Officer/Aviation Engineering Duty Officer

Engineering duty officers (EDO) are involved in the design, construction, and repair of ships, submarines, and systems related to naval warfare. All EDOs start their careers as line officers. After obtaining operational experience, interested officers may apply for conversion to EDO through the semiannual transfer/redesignation board. New SWO and submarine officers with exceptional academic records may apply for the engineering duty (ED) option upon commissioning. If selected for the ED option, you will be transferred to the EDO community upon warfare qualification and completion of your first division officer tour. More information is available at the BUPERS EDO Web site: http://www.npc.navy.mil/Officer/Pers44/EngineeringDuty/.

Full-Time Support
Full-time support (FTS) officers are reserve officers on active duty who perform duties in connection with organizing, administering, recruiting, and training of Navy Reserve components. FTS officers provide support to the Navy Reserve in the areas of manpower management, administration, mobilization, logistics, financial management, and facilities management. The FTS community is filled through the semiannual transfer/redesignation board from virtually all other officer communities. The FTS Community Manager site includes additional information: http://www.npc.navy.mil/Officer/CommunityManagers/ReserveBranch/FullTimeSupport/.

Human Resource Professional
Human resource (HR) officers fill the need for professional administrators of the Navy's complex personnel management system. HRs serve on fleet, joint, and naval headquarters staffs, and within the Bureau of Naval Personnel. These officers enter their community through the lateral transfer/redesignation process either at the O-2/3 level, if they do not have significant HR experience, or at the O-4 level with significant HR experience. More info can be obtained at http://www.npc.navy.mil/Officer/Pers44/HumanResources/.

Oceanography
Oceanography special duty assignment officers enter through the lateral transfer/redesignation path after earning a warfare qualification in one of the line communities. Oceanographers work within nine warfare directorates that support operational commanders, and they frequently specialize in areas such as physical oceanography or meteorology. Oceanographers are assigned to one of the fleet meteorological centers, major staffs, or research and development organizations. The BUPERS oceanography site offers extensive information: http://www.npc.navy.mil/Officer/Pers44/OCEANO/.

Information Professional, Information Warfare, and Intelligence Officers
Information professional officers (IP), information warfare officers (IW), and intelligence officers (IO) either enter through the lateral transfer process or, less frequently, are commissioned directly into one of these

communities from the Naval Academy, Officer Candidate School (OCS), or Reserve Officers' Training Corps (ROTC). Information professionals provide a cadre of experienced computer network and radio communications specialists to support warfighting requirements. IPs serve at sea on large ships, on major staffs, at naval telecommunications centers around the world, and on acquisition projects.

Information warfare special duty assignment officers manage electronic warfare, signals intelligence, and cryptological functions for the Navy and on joint assignments. They work on major and joint staffs, at sea on larger ships, at cryptologic resource centers, at one of the three joint intelligence centers, and on related acquisition programs. Intelligence special duty assignment officers serve as analysts and interpreters, providing intelligence support on staffs, large ships, aircraft squadrons, special warfare groups, and to the joint intelligence centers. The Web sites for these communities can be found at the BUPERS IP Web site: http:// www.npc.navy.mil/Officer/Intelligence_Information/.

Foreign Area Officer
The foreign area officer (FAO) is a relatively new field that has emerged in recognition of the need for officers with extensive experience in specific geographic regions. According to the BUPERS FAO Web site, "Once selected for FAO and then assigned a region, officers can expect language training at DLI [Defense Language Institute] and academic training at NPS [Naval Postgraduate School]. One to six months of In Country Immersion Training will be the final phase of FAO training to hone language and cultural skills." FAOs serve on staffs of fleets, combatant commands, and defense agencies as well as in DoD military-diplomatic offices at U.S. embassies and diplomatic posts. All FAOs must be warfare qualified and enter through the lateral transfer process. The FAO page discusses the requirements and purpose of this new field: http://www.npc.navy.mil/ Officer/Expeditionary_Warfare/ForeignArea/.

Public Affairs Officer
Public affairs officers (PAO) serve throughout the Navy, promoting our message and supporting naval command staffs. Public affairs officers attend the Defense Information School (DINFOS) at Fort Meade, Maryland, prior to their first duty station. This ten-week course covers the principles of public information and community relations as well as Department of Defense policies. PAOs serve with combat camera units, with the Navy News organization, and on all major and joint staffs. The PAO page on the BUPERS site includes additional information: http://www.npc.navy.mil/

Officer/Expeditionary_Warfare/PublicAffairs/.

Limited Duty Officer/Chief Warrant Officer

Limited duty officers (LDO) and chief warrant officers (CWO) are drawn from the enlisted force and are commissioned to act as technical managers and provide deck-plate leadership. LDOs and CWOs are commissioned with a designator that is closely aligned with their prior enlisted rate. Because each designator is so narrowly focused, each has a unique career path. Fortunately, each designator has a Web page that lies within their broad parent community (surface warfare, aviation, submarine, or special warfare). The LDO/CWO Officer Community Manager page has links to each community: http://www.npc.navy.mil/Officer/CommunityManagers/LDOCWOOCM/.

Restricted Line Communities

Restricted line, or staff, communities function in support of the unrestricted line and the Navy as a whole. The explanations given here provide an entry point for further exploration of each of the Staff Corps communities.

Chaplain Corps

Chaplains initially go through six weeks of training at the U.S. Navy Chaplain School, located in Newport, Rhode Island, and may attend several additional courses before being ordered to an operational ministry. A viable career in the Chaplain Corps will include a variety of tours—operational, overseas, hospital, staff, and with the Marine Corps. Chaplain detailers advise career-minded chaplains not to stay in one geographical area for too long and—as with any other naval career—taking the "hard" assignment counts. The U.S. Navy Chaplain Web site can provide more information on this service community: http://www.chaplain.navy.mil/.

Judge Advocate General Corps

U.S. Navy judge advocate generals (JAG) practice criminal prosecution and defense, provide legal assistance to U.S. Navy and Marine Corps members, and assist naval commands. The JAG Corps is manned through direct accession as well as with officers from the unrestricted line who were selected for legal training. Direct appointment officers must be graduates of a law school accredited by the American Bar Association and must be admitted to practice by either federal court or the highest court of a state. Officer candidates attend a six-week indoctrination course at the Officer Development School in Newport, Rhode Island, followed by Naval Justice School. A great deal of information can be found on the Navy JAG Web site: http://

www.jag.navy.mil; and at the NPC site: http://www.npc.navy.mil/Officer/
Pers44/JAGCorps/.

Medical/Dental Communities
Navy medicine includes the Medical Corps, Dental Corps, Medical
Service Corps, and Nurse Corps. Each is staffed through direct acces-
sions and through in-service procurement programs from the enlisted and
officer ranks of the Navy. Direct commission officers may be inducted at
an advanced rank, depending on education and experience. New officers
will attend the five-week Officer Development School in Newport, Rhode
Island. The Navy Bureau of Medicine site may be consulted for more
information on the great variety of subspecialties in the Navy's medical
community: http://navymedicine.med.navy.mil/bumed/index.cfm.

Supply Corps Officer
The Supply Corps constitutes one of the largest staff communities in the
Navy. Supply officers serve on ships, submarines, and in aviation units
around the world. Supply officers generally specialize in a primary warfare
community (surface, subsurface, or air) and will further subspecialize in
a particular field such as acquisition or fuels management. New officers
attend the Navy Supply Corps School in Athens, Georgia, for roughly
six months. Initial training includes the supply officer basic course, division officer leadership, and community specialization. The Supply Corps
School maintains an excellent Web site that has a wealth of information:
https://www.netc.navy.mil/centers/css/nscs/default.cfm.

Following initial training, you will report to an operational unit to
serve as a division officer. Here you will likely earn your warfare specialty,
such as the surface warfare supply corps officer (SWSCO) pin. The first
operational tour is often followed by a tour at a shore facility such as
one of the major Fleet Industrial Supply Centers (FISC). Many officers
will earn an advanced degree during their first shore tour, then go on to
second operational tour as a department head. Senior level tours include
management of major programs, sea tours on large ships such as aircraft carriers, and command of one of the many supply activities around
the world. The Bureau of Naval Personnel PERS-44 Supply Corps page
is http://www.npc.navy.mil/Officer/Pers44/SupplyCorps/. Of particular interest is the "It's Your Career" document, a PDF file found in the
Career Counselor section.
Civil Engineer Corps

Civil Engineer Corps (CEC) officers serve on major staffs and manage large construction projects around the world. They are uniformed professional architects and engineers who work in contracting, public works, and construction and who run the Navy's construction battalions. CEC officers enter through ROTC, OCS, or lateral transfer. Newly commissioned CEC officers attend the basic course at the Civil Engineer Corps Officer School (CECOS) in Port Hueneme, California. The basic course consists of eight weeks of CEC orientation along with five weeks of basic government contracting principles for a total of thirteen weeks. All career-oriented CEC officers will attend graduate school somewhere between their fourth and tenth years of service. The BUPERS CEC Web site includes more information: http://www.npc.navy.mil/Officer/Expeditionary_Warfare/CivilEngineerCorps/.

Career Management

All organizations have an embedded culture that values certain attributes and experiences in their employees, and the Navy is no different. Certain highly talented individuals will do well anywhere, but for most of us, an understanding of what the Navy expects from us goes a long way toward ensuring career success. This section will introduce you to some of those expectations. The first (and always foremost) of these criteria is "sustained superior performance."

Sustained Superior Performance

Your performance in demanding operational assignments is the basic currency of promotion and career milestone screening. For most officer communities, this translates into a frequently heard phrase, "sustained superior performance at sea." At every stage of your career, your commanding officer will document your performance in an annual fitness report. Once you reach the rank of lieutenant, you will be competitively evaluated against your peers at your command (for LDOs and CWOs this competitive evaluation begins immediately). A note of caution: While breaking out ahead of your peers will be favorable to your career, teamwork and your willingness to help others are highly important—placing your own career above the good of the command or at the expense of your peers is not the way to get ahead.

Community and Pentagon Tours

All officer communities will expect you to fulfill "community tours" in addition to your operational tours. These are the jobs that make the Navy and your specific service community run—jobs in major acquisition programs, detailing jobs in Millington, or OPNAV tours (working on the staff supporting the Chief of Naval Operations [CNO] at the Pentagon). While these jobs may seem far away from your core operational profession, they are vital to the smooth operation of the Navy and are recognized as such by promotion and selection boards. For most officers, these assignments come after your department head tours. Not all successful officers spend time in Washington, but your long-term career will likely benefit when you do (although excellence in the fleet remains the most important driver in your career).

Advanced Education

Most officer communities strongly encourage their officers to earn a master's degree. In some communities, a lack of advanced education may negatively affect your competitiveness as your reach command screening gates (check with your mentors to see how things work in your community). Fortunately, the Navy has a wide range of advanced education options available, including the Naval Postgraduate School in Monterey, California; the Naval War College in Newport, Rhode Island; and a wide variety of full-time, overseas scholarship, and off-duty options. Most degrees will lead to your being awarded a subspecialty code, which may determine what jobs you will be detailed to in the future. The Bureau's Education/Training Placement page provides additional information on educational opportunities for officers: http://www.npc.navy.mil/Officer/Education_Placement/.

Joint Professional Military Education

Joint professional military education (JPME) is required for all military officers, regardless of branch of service. JPME phase 1 must be completed prior to your command screening board (JPME phase 2 is required later in your career). This requirement was levied by the 1984 Goldwater–Nichols Defense Reorganization Act to enhance joint (i.e., multiservice) warfighting capability. JPME phase 1 consists of three courses (strategy and war, joint maritime operations, and national decision making) that on average take about one year to complete and can be earned via correspondence course or in residence at a war college. The BUPERS Joint Officer page has more information: http://www.npc.navy.mil/Officer/JointOfficer/Joint+Credit+Requirements.htm.

Managing Your Record

In a very real sense, what your service record says on paper (or, more accurately these days, on the screen) *is* you. Your promotion prospects, future assignments, and screening for major milestones such as command at sea all rely on what is in your service record. Your service record resides at the

Bureau of Naval Personnel in Millington, Tennessee. The Navy does a fairly good job of maintaining your record, but only you can make sure that it truly reflects all of the good things you've done in your career.

Two documents to pay attention to are your officer data card (ODC) and your performance summary record (PSR). These online records are available only through the BUPERS On-Line (BOL) portal with a password or common access card (CAC). The ODC includes your service history or OSR (officer service record), which lists all past duty assignments, education, personal data, subspecialty codes, and qualifications. The PSR lists all of your fitness reports. It provides the date, command, grades, and the reporting senior's trait average, which allows you to compare your performance against other officers your boss has evaluated.

The BOL site also allows you to order a compact disk that contains your complete service record, called an official military personnel file (OMPF). Savvy officers order theirs once per year to check that all documents are accounted for. There is also a handy board preparation checklist included that covers most service-record maintenance issues.

Switching Communities

Most officers in support communities come from the three main line communities through the lateral transfer/redesignation board, which meets twice per year. Officers choose to apply for redesignation for a number of reasons, including interest, family concerns, or better career potential in a different field. This process is competitive, and each board selects the best-qualified officers for each community, taking into account both the needs of the gaining community and the candidate's existing community. Options for redesignation include:

★ Aerospace engineering duty officer
★ Engineering duty officer
★ Human resources professional
★ Information professional
★ Intelligence
★ Information warfare
★ Public affairs
★ Foreign area officer
★ Oceanography
★ Civil Engineer Corps
★ Medical Service Corps
★ Full-time support
    There is also the opportunity to transfer between line communities

(for instance, a few officers from other communities are selected for pilot training each year), or to one of the staff corps communities, such as supply. Refer to the BUPERS Lateral Transfer/Redesignation page for more information: http://www.npc.navy.mil/Boards/Administrative/ActiveDutyTransferRedesignation/.

Conclusion

Nothing can take the place of solid advice from your CO, other mentors, and your detailer, but the principles presented here are universal: Sustained superior performance in operational billets and the effective management of the expected requirements of your respective service community are essential building blocks to a successful naval career.

Recommended References

Bureau of Naval Personnel Web site: http://www.npc.navy.mil/channels. The Navy's online source for career information.

Career Compass by James A. Winnefeld (Naval Institute Press, 2005). An outstanding book of advice for the career-minded military officer.

★ 10 ★

ADVICE FOR NAVY SPOUSES

Welcome to the Navy! While your husband or wife is entering the Navy, you play an equally important part in this journey; there is no doubt that as a spouse, or a future spouse, you are entering a new and exciting world as well.

Being a member of a Navy family holds incredible promise for travel, interesting places to live, and camaraderie. It also brings the challenges of absence and the adjustment to a lifestyle that will be different from other walks of life. Simply put, military spouses also sacrifice and serve, and it is not surprising that the first person most military service members credit for their success is their spouse.

The goal of this chapter is to provide the spouse of the newly commissioned officer a short introduction to life in the Navy. For a more comprehensive view of marriage and family life in the Navy, please refer to the *Navy Spouse's Guide* by Laura Hall Stavridis (Naval Institute Press, 2002), a truly exceptional book that provides far more detailed and broader advice for those who are married to a member of the U.S. Navy. Another title, *Homefront Club: The Hardheaded Woman's Guide to Raising a Military Family* by Jacey Eckart (Naval Institute Press, 2005), offers "married-but-single parents" practical advice laced with humor to address the unique challenges faced by military spouses.

Evolving Roles

No organization, including the Navy, is perfect, but you can take heart that today's spouse does not face the life of white linens and lace that has often been unfairly associated with the social life (and hierarchy) of Navy spouses of the past. Although there are wonderful military spouses from previous generations who thoroughly enjoyed their lives in the military family, today the advent of the two-career family and a general loosening in formality have made the life of a spouse less formal, if no less demanding.

Today's Navy recognizes that spouses, particularly the spouses of more junior naval personnel, often have careers of their own. As society has evolved to adjust to both spouses working outside the home, so has the Navy. Many officers, including COs and XOs, will have spouses who have careers of their own, and you will also encounter naval peers who are geographic bachelors with their families living in another town.

These changes have resulted in spouses having more latitude regarding whether to participate in the social interactions with other Navy spouses. Those who do will share a common experience, likely have more fun, and will have resources and networks they can rely on when they face the inevitable challenges that military family life can occasionally bring. The spouses who choose not to participate may find their experience as a Navy spouse less collaborative and enjoyable—like most things in life, having good friends to share challenges with often makes the experience more positive. The good news is that the days of spouses being mentioned in service members' performance evaluations are long gone, so today those who participate do so because of an honest desire to make friends and share experiences.

While the words and titles that are unique to the military may at first seem very intimidating, just as in the civilian world, respect, consideration, and humility go a long way. Because the Navy is such a mobile profession where absence is a part of life, you will find most naval groups and families very welcoming—we all understand what it is like to be the new person, and most military families go out of their way to help the newly arrived feel welcome.

Terms

There are several books that feature larger glossaries of naval terms including the *Navy Spouse's Guide*; here are a few terms to get you started. Some other sources might have more precise definitions, but these equip you with a basic understanding of terms you will hear often from your military member and more experienced spouses:

★ *Deployment*—Period of time in which operational commands serve away from home.

★ *Wardroom*—Term used to describe the officers in a command; stems from the space on ships where officers traditionally meet and dine.

★ *Ready Room*—Term used to describe the officers in an aviation squadron, as well as the space on an aircraft carrier where the aviators conduct their flight briefs and normal everyday business while at sea.

★ *Commissary*—Supermarket on base that only military and their family members can patronize.

★ *Exchange, or PX*—Department store on base that only military and their family members can patronize.

★ *Duty*—Period of time in which naval personnel are required to stay at a command (potentially overnight) to provide security or administrative support.

★ *Leave*—All naval personnel are afforded thirty days of leave per year. Leave is requested formally though a leave request form or "leave chit." In commands that are operational (ships, squadrons, submarines, special warfare commands), leave plans will need to be balanced against operational or deployment schedules.

★ *Liberty*—When naval personnel are not deployed, liberty is granted at the end of the current workday until the commencement of the next workday.

★ *Inspection/Assessment*—An on-site visit to a command conducted by off-ship experts to evaluate a particular competency or mission area. In many cases, a command's ability to deploy depends on a successful assessment, so preparations before an inspection or assessment may require more work and time from your family's service member.

Social Events

Hail and Farewell

As an organization that sees perpetual rotation of personnel, the Hail and Farewell has few comparable events in civilian careers. Generally intended for the wardroom and its spouses only, the event's main purpose is to "hail," or welcome, new members and their spouses and bid farewell to those leaving. Other than those broad outlines, however, the atmosphere can be as varied as the types of commands in the Navy. These events can range from roasts of those departing all the way to a very sincere but sedate reception.

As in any event related to gathering with coworkers, moderation in consuming food and alcohol is always a sound strategy, and you should never feel compelled to consume alcohol if you prefer not to. In many Hail and Farewells, spouses are also recognized and other spouses may be asked to say a few words. As a newer spouse or significant other, you will have few formal responsibilities other than having a nice time and getting to know some of your spouse's new coworkers and their husbands and wives.

Wetting Down

One of the most enjoyable customs in the Navy is the wetting down. Naval lore suggests that those officers who have been recently promoted dedicate their first paycheck to celebrate their advancement with their shipmates in a gathering known as "wetting down." Today's realities of family and finances usually make these celebrations more humble affairs with junior officers often teaming up to host a combined wetting down. Although these events may be limited to officers only, spouses are often invited as well.

Social Outings for Spouses
Particularly during deployments or extended absences, the Family Readiness Group, a volunteer organization of spouses at a given command, may host events as varied as Halloween parties for the command's children or Half-Way Deployment celebration nights. On a less formal scale, the spouses of commissioned officers may also choose to get together for a low-key dinner or event. Once again, these events are in no way mandatory, but they will build the relationships that will help sustain you during the times while your spouse or significant other is away.

Military Celebrations
Once or twice a year you will have the opportunity to attend a Navy Birthday Ball or a ball for your spouse's military community. These events are not inexpensive, but they are usually priced to be a bit more affordable for the more junior members of the community and are most enjoyable when you have a large group of friends and shipmates going together. If it is within your budget, consider staying at the hotel where the event is being hosted. There are often discount rooms available, and making this decision extends the experience and protects both you and your spouse from driving home if you have consumed alcohol, although there is no requirement for you to consume alcoholic beverages at today's naval events.

RSVPs
Just as in your own social life, you will receive invitations for events that the host is hoping for you to attend but is counting on your consideration to indicate whether you accept or decline the invitation. Food, service, and a myriad of other details can hang in the balance while the host attempts to calculate the number of guests. Many a host has been frustrated by those who fail to respond promptly to an invitation. Be considerate and do not be the person who inconveniences a prospective host by not responding to an invitation.

Leadership Roles to Understand
Commanding Officer
The commanding officer is often referred to as the CO, captain, or, in some communities, "skipper" (ask your spouse what is customary at his or her command) and is the leader of your husband's or wife's command. These leaders carry a responsibility and accountability that in many ways run profoundly deeper than those of a civilian chief executive officer. At sea, these leaders carry particularly significant responsibilities for every aspect of their command's well-being and combat performance, but whether your spouse's first command is at sea or ashore, these career leaders warrant your courtesy and respect.

When you are introduced to your spouse's commanding officer, it is perfectly fine to respond, "Pleased to meet you, Commander Jones," and then move on to general conversation. Those spouses who are not in the military themselves may be invited by the commanding officer to refer to him or her by first name, and if that is the case, feel free to do so. While commanding officers will be deeply interested in how your spouse is adjusting to his chosen career, remember that, depending on the size of command, the CO's contact with your spouse may vary. Depending on the size and style of event, the commanding officer will likely be interested in conversing with a number of people, so once you have a chance to exchange pleasantries and brief conversation, be respectful of the CO's time and the other guests at the event who may be interested in communicating with him or her as well.

Commanding Officer's Spouse
Although spousal roles have evolved over the years, there is no mistaking that there is still a leadership role to be played by the CO's spouse. This role will vary greatly due to many circumstances (the spouse's profession, whether the spouse is colocated, the spouse's personal style and preferences, and so on). Regardless of the details, in the vast majority of situations the CO's spouse will play a significant role in your command's family and social leadership.

Executive Officer
The executive officer, or XO, the second most senior officer at a command, will be in charge of the administrative and training needs of your spouse's command. Depending on the division of labor at the command (and the desires of the commanding officer) the XO may be very heavily involved in the development of junior officers. If the commanding officer is unmarried or a geographic bachelor, the XO's spouse may be the recognized leader in the wardroom community as well.

Command Master Chief

The command master chief (CMC) is the third member of the command triad. Charged with the care and development of all enlisted Sailors in the command, he plays a prominent role in the command and is an incredible source of knowledge and experience. If your spouse is assigned responsibility for enlisted Sailors as a division officer, for example, the CMC will likely figure prominently in any quality-of-life issues faced by enlisted Sailors.

Command Master Chief's Spouse

Like the CO's spouse, the husband or wife of the CMC is generally viewed as holding a position of leadership among the community of families at a given command. Once again, this role will vary based on personal experiences, but the vast majority of these spouses are superb sources of experience and advice in their own right.

Department Head

While middle managers are often humorously maligned in popular culture, they are vital to well-run organizations, and the Navy is no exception. In most operational naval organizations, your spouse's first line manager will be the department head. While the relationships between the spouses of naval officers are far less formal and hierarchal, you will often find that the department head's spouse will be another valuable source of help and advice.

Ombudsman

The ombudsman, appointed by the CO, is the official conduit between the command and the families. These very important leaders are vital to a healthy command and family community climate and they are critical connections for families looking for general information or for those facing specific challenges. If your command is one that deploys, the ombudsman will often maintain a phone message system known as the Care Line, which informs families of a deployed command's status and news.

Family and Financial Matters

Pay

Just as you likely experienced when you viewed your first civilian paycheck, you will see a number of entries and deductions related to your partner's pay on his or her first naval paycheck. The vast majority of the military's pay system can be accessed through the program MyPay; a more in-depth description of the Navy's pay system is in chapter 6 of this book. Much of this information is protected by passwords, and your spouse's permission is required for you to access pay information. If your military member deploys or is away for an extended period, you may need a power of attorney to make broader financial decisions and actions (your spouse's command can help your spouse and you to arrange for this).

Family Emergency Planning
As September 11, 2001, and Hurricane Katrina have tragically reminded our nation, having a plan for crisis is important. When facing the specter of a man-made or natural incident, it is important to have a plan for your family. The government site www.ready.gov provides exceptional advice for a family's personal readiness plan. The *Navy Spouse's Guide* includes a complete description of the papers and material you should have ready access to on short notice. The Navy also has a robust tool known as Operation Prepare, which helps service members and their families plan for emergency response during national emergencies and disasters. See https://www.cnic.navy.mil/CNIC_HQ_Site/OpPrepare/index.htm.

Dependent Identification Cards
Your military dependent identification card is the form of identification that is most crucial to your being able to access military support. This ID card will be required for you to enter a naval base, use the commissary and exchange, and enjoy the many other amenities on a base such as the gyms, MWR facilities, and so on. Safeguarding this card is critical, and replacing lost ID cards can be difficult (particularly when the naval member is away from home port), so treat this card with a care that equals or exceeds the care you take in handling your credit cards and driver's license.

The subject of dependent ID cards points to another topic that has frustrated many *future* spouses of military officers. Given the considerable access and financial benefits that these ID cards provide and because of security considerations, fiancées are not issued military ID cards. This can prove logistically challenging for someone who no doubt plays an important role in his or her future spouse's life, but this should be anticipated and planned for.

Moving
Moving is a constant in the military profession (and in many other competitive leadership fields in the civilian world), and the Navy has made great strides in making the moving process more transparent and easier to plan. For a thorough description of the process, visit the web site http://www.smartwebmove.navsup.navy.mil. Remember that to arrange a move in the Navy, you will need a copy of your spouse's military orders, the document that directs your spouse to transfer from one military assignment to another.

Despite the fact that the planning process has become a bit more streamlined, moves are still major family undertakings that generally occur every two to three years in a military family's life. Planning ahead and good communication among the military member, the military spouse, and the command are essential to keep the stress related to this process at a minimum. Many experienced military families have moving binders and files to collect all the required information and receipts; you should seek out their advice as well as that of the Household Goods Office at your closest naval installation.

Visiting Your Loved One's Ship/Command

Just as there are appropriate times for your service member to visit you at your workplace, there are appropriate times to visit your naval member's command. Most commands will have clear visiting policies during the day and during the weekends. It is best to check the policy and avoid dropping by without notice. Many operational commands can be inherently busy and sometimes dangerous to someone unfamiliar with the environment, so there are good reasons for these limitations. Additionally, just like your workplace, ships and commands are focused on getting the job done during the day.

Family Day or Cruise

Some of the great memories of military family life stem from occasions when military commands share their activities with family members. Usually once a year or so, depending on operational schedule, your service member's command will invite families to visit the ship or command for the Navy's version of an open house. For surface ships, this may include a cruise where the ship actually gets under way for a short time. These can be very memorable days and attendance is highly encouraged, but planning, preparation, and abiding by the command policies are essential to providing for the best experience for your family. Note that these occasions are often less frequent in naval activities that are more shore-based or administrative in nature, but other events such as family picnics or command events such as holiday parties will also be available for most military family members to enjoy.

Staying Connected

Your ability to communicate with your newly commissioned officer varies with his or her military assignment. In many training commands where ensigns report initially, they will often not have direct phone lines, and the most you will be able to do is leave a message. If you are one of the lucky spouses who have military members with their their own desks and phones, remember to use this judiciously because your recently commissioned officer will likely have a busy workload day in and day out. Even though your spouse may have a personal cell phone, the nature of his or her work may preclude a cell phone during work hours.

E-mail is often the most reliable way to convey routine information to a military family member. Although your spouse will have many duties during the day, most will have opportunity to review e-mail several times per day. You should not be alarmed or disappointed, however, if your military loved one does not answer your e-mails in a near instantaneous fashion—particularly if he or she is in an operational or deployed status. You may be initially frustrated that the Navy's lifestyle does not align with a "9-to-5" desk job experience, but you will soon develop a communications rhythm with your spouse. Due to security concerns, be mindful that official movement of a command cannot be disclosed via normal means, including e-mail.

Communications capabilities have rapidly evolved in the Navy and, fortunately, the days of military families solely communicating by posted letter every two weeks are long gone. Even when your loved ones are overseas or under way, they will be able to receive e-mail the vast majority of the time. In some cases, phone calls will also be possible at sea, but recognize that "voice communications" are a much rarer commodity at sea, so do not expect many calls. If you do receive a phone call, expect it to be fairly short because there will likely be other Sailors waiting to call their families as well. When your deployed spouse has the chance for liberty overseas, however, opportunities for phone calls are much more plentiful, so consider purchasing appropriate international calling cards before your spouse deploys.

Separations and Reunions

Long absences from your loved one are never easy, and deployments and other highly demanding periods are a fact of life for the newly commissioned officer and his or her family. The Navy Fleet and Family Support Center, located in most fleet areas of concentrations, are wonderful resources for families dealing with separation; representatives from these centers will often visit with your returning military family member on transits home following a deployment.

The challenge of separation when a loved one is on deployment is obvious, but reunions can often pose their own challenges. Just as the military member has likely changed a bit on deployment, you and your family may have changed as well. The spouse who has remained at home has likely been used to making more decisions unilaterally, and the children may now be used to dealing with just one parental authority figure. Successfully

For more than two hundred years, homecomings have been special for the U.S. Navy and our families. (U.S. Navy, MC3 Joshua Rodriguez)

reincorporating a second adult figure into a household following a six- to nine-month absence is a process that requires hard work, communication, and an understanding that everyone in the family will require some time to adjust and grow following a long awaited reunion.

Expectations regarding what will occur during a returning officer's first day home are often the first point at which a divergence of your respective visions can occur—if you are not communicating. Individual preferences vary, but often the military member returning from deployment is most interested in spending a quiet day with family at home while the military spouse—after remaining behind to singly manage the house, the family, and often a professional career as well—is anxious to celebrate and reunite outside the confines of the home. Once again, with most post-deployment periods affording navy personnel a week or two of leave, a good plan and good communication should enable both partners to meet their expectations.

Challenges and Rewards

Married and family life in the Navy offers many challenges and rewards. Although the challenges of separation, changing schedules, and the potential of your spouse going into harm's way all exist, you and your family will also have incredible experiences that include travel, living in many

103

exciting areas throughout the country and the world, and the camaraderie of other great families who have chosen to support their loved ones' calling to serve their nation. Navy spouses and families also serve and sacrifice, but the rewards and satisfaction that await those who do are often extraordinary. If both partners remember to remain flexible and thoughtful, their efforts will help to smooth all transitions—moving, deploying, separating, or reuniting.

★ 11 ★

BASIC NAVAL MANAGEMENT

Regardless of what community you join as you begin your first job as a commissioned officer, things will get moving pretty quickly, particularly if you are immediately reporting to an assignment that involves management responsibilities. Even if your first tour as an officer is in a training command, many of these management tips will be relevant no matter when you take on your first job in the fleet.

Initially you may wonder what your job is, what resources are available to you, and what special activities, training, and missions you are responsible for. Fortunately, there will be other people at your command who have done your job (or a very similar one) before you. Additionally, just as in other elements of life in the Navy, there are references that will guide you regarding the requirements and procedures related to your job. So whether you are starting your first job on a deployment or during a maintenance period, managing a well-run division or one that needs some work—you are not alone as you begin this challenge.

Turnover

Turnover, the process of one individual turning over a responsibility to another, is a concept that permeates many aspects of naval leadership and life. In a tactical situation, Sailors of all ranks conduct a turnover with their predecessors before assuming a watch position. Similarly, when one leader takes responsibility for an organization (whether it is a squad, work center, division, or command), the requirement for a good turnover is equally important.

Commanding officers and flag officers often dedicate a week or more to conducting a turnover before taking charge of the commands they will lead. Similarly, whether you are a traditional division officer at sea or in a more administrative position, you will likely spend a few days with the person whose management responsibilities you will inherit. For those turning over for the first time, there will be a lot of information presented and not a lot of time to process it—the managerial equivalent of "drinking from a fire hose."

The person you relieve should be able to give you a good review of all programs you will manage, the material condition of all spaces and equipment you will be responsible for, and your part in any upcoming assessments or missions that your command will undertake. It is imperative that you ask questions and take notes. Polite, detailed questions are appropriate, but this is not the time to tell your predecessor how you would do things. Be respectful of the experience and effort of the person turning over to you—do not be critical or identify things you are going to change. Your purpose is to gain an overall understanding of the organization you are going to lead and manage.

Questions to Ask
It is highly likely that you will be given a turnover notebook or briefing, but there are a few basic questions to have in your hip pocket. If you do not understand a term or acronym, ask the person to stop and explain—every person in the Navy was new once and will understand your lack of familiarity with certain terms. If it is not possible to ask your questions right away, write them down to ask later. Here are some examples of good questions to ask:

★ What spaces/buildings/equipment are you responsible for? (You should visit every room or space in the organization you are responsible for.)
★ What programs are you responsible for?
★ How are the divisional/squad/unit responsibilities divided up?
★ Are there any ongoing personnel issues you should be aware of?
★ Who are your primary points of contact for each area you are responsible for? (internal to your command as well as external)
★ What publications and instructions are applicable to your area(s) of responsibility? Which ones have been most helpful?
★ What unit/ship-level instructions are you responsible for?
★ Are there any collateral duties related to your primary job that you will be responsible for?
★ What schools or enlisted manning are required for this division or unit? Are there any current or projected shortfalls?
★ What training or exercises are required? How do you track them?
★ What events in the next three to six months in the command schedule is your organization responsible for? How are preparations for those events coming?

Taking Notes

Just as with a lecture in high school or college, you will not be able to retain everything that is passed on to you by sheer memory. Be sure to keep a notebook with you at all times. As you process the information you write down, do not hesitate to jot down additional questions as you think of them. Even after you are done turning over, keep your notes—you will find yourself referring to them well after the turnover process, and when it comes time for you to turn over these duties to the next young officer in a year or two, they will be a superb tool as you prepare for the transfer.

As you go through this process, the person you are relieving should show you where things are. The publications and instructions that outline the requirements for your job should be easily accessible. Remember, there is a reference for the vast majority of managerial challenges in the Navy—even how to inspect a space or office. There should be copies of the command's instructions for you to review as well as information on required maintenance, personnel status, and documentation of all ongoing maintenance. You will probably not have time to review these references during turnover, but you will want to get familiar with them shortly thereafter.

Completing the Turnover

While it is not always required, you may have to route a turnover letter. Once that letter is signed by the commanding officer, you're it! Any significant issues—whether in the material status of gear you will now be responsible for or personnel issues that will affect your organization—should be in this letter.

In some commands, this turnover concludes very simply with you reporting to your immediate boss (often your department head) while in other environments you may be expected to personally report to a more senior officer to notify him or her that you have assumed duties. If this is the case, ask your predecessor or other officers what is expected—you may be asked a few questions by the captain or executive officer to assess your knowledge of your new organization.

Talk with your chief and leading petty officer as well as your department head before completing the turnover process to ensure you have covered all the necessary information. While your predecessor may be the primary person you will first receive information from, he or she will soon depart, so be sure to also interface with the enlisted personnel you will be working with over the long term since they will be your teammates over the tenure of your first job.

19 Jan 06

From: ENS Sara J. Green, USNR, 123-45-6789/1110
To: Commanding Officer, USS FASTSHIP
Via: (1) ENS Joshua M. Smith, USN, 456-78-9123/1110
(2) Engineering Officer, USS FASTSHIP
(3) Executive Officer, USS FASTSHIP

Subj: REPORT OF RELIEF AS ELECTRICAL OFFICER

Ref: (a) OPNAVINST 3120.32C, NAVY SORM
(b) FASTSHIPINST 3120.1A, FASTSHIP SORM

1. As of this date, I have officially relieved ENS Joshua Smith of all duties as Electrical Officer in USS FASTSHIP.

2. ENS Smith and I have jointly reviewed the records and programs under the cognizance of the Electrical Officer, as described in references (a) and (b). The status of those items is as follows:

a) **Condition of all electrical equipment**. I have assessed the condition of all equipment under the Electrical Officer's cognizance and I find it in satisfactory condition with the exceptions noted in Engineering Department's Eight O'clock Reports.

b) **Supervision and training of watchstanders**. All critical watch stations under the cognizant control of the Electrical Officer are adequately manned, trained, and supervised.

c) **Material condition and cleanliness**. A walk-through of all spaces was conducted. Condition and cleanliness of all EE Division spaces is satisfactory with the exception of the electrical grade matting in the Tool Issue Room.

3. I accept all duties and responsibilities as Electical Officer.

Sara J. Green
Sara J. Green
ENS   USN

Managing Your Division

With the fast pace of operational tasking and the need for your command to be surge-ready, once the person you have relieved has departed, you will likely find yourself very busy keeping up with all the requirements and tasking (or assignments) coming your way. This challenge will be compounded by the personal qualifications you will be required to start working on and any collateral jobs or duties you may be assigned.

Your division will be responsible for many items. If you attempt to directly tend to each item, you will quickly become overwhelmed. Your chief and leading petty officer will help you delegate and respond to tasking and traditionally assign individual responsibilities and tasks to the Sailors in your division of organization. As a junior officer, part of your job is to help bring a broader perspective to your division as you lead them.

Starting the Day
In most commands, ashore or afloat, you will be required to attend some sort of morning meeting. In commands where you have leadership responsibilities, you will likely attend a meeting for officers and chiefs followed by a meeting with your Sailors. In many commands, this initial morning meeting for all officers and chiefs is called officer's call or khaki call.

Whether it is the XO or another high-ranking officer that runs this meeting, he or she will provide information about future events, outstanding requirements, and a laundry list of other information. Depending on how your command is organized, you may find yourself at another short meeting where the department head goes over his or her task list. The daily guidance you receive from your XO and department head will help you maintain the big picture, and it will be your job to keep your division informed and ensure they will be ready to support the ship for future events. Remember to write down tasking! Not only are you looking out for the ship, you are taking care of your people by identifying and prioritizing their tasks.

Divisional Leadership Positions
Within your division, there will be people assigned to take care of different divisional responsibilities. Some examples of this are:

★ Leading chief petty officer (LCPO)—The leading chief in your division and your main leadership partner.
★ Leading petty officer (LPO)—Your senior petty officer, usually a first-class petty officer.
★ Workcenter supervisor (WCS)—A mid-tier petty officer, usually an E-5, who is charged with leading one of your division's work centers.
★ Maintenance personnel—The remainder of your Sailors who perform the maintenance on the systems and equipment associated with your division.

Just as you will likely be assigned collateral duties, there are many divisional level collateral duties assigned to your personnel. While these duties

Not all management in the Navy involves paperwork. Here an ensign relays information during a training exercise. (U.S. Navy, PHAN Lamel J. Hinton)

are divisional in nature, they are also command-wide programs, so your Sailor who fills a collateral duty will likely be receiving guidance from the command's program manager. These jobs may include a safety petty officer; training petty officer; a morale, welfare, and recreation representative; and an electrical safety petty officer. You should make sure that your Sailors are fulfilling their collateral duties as well. If you take the view that any collateral duty held by someone in your division or unit is in many ways yours as well, you will take a big step in ensuring the success of your division and your personnel.

Growing on the Job

The longer you hold a position, the more sure-footed you will become regarding your responsibilities. For now, your focus should be on learning the basics of your divisional responsibilities and building a relationship with your leading chief petty officer. These items should go hand in hand because your LCPO will play a significant role in training you how to manage a division. While individual strengths and weaknesses will dictate what this relationship looks like, one of the keys to success is to go to your chief first.

Remember to be firm, fair, and consistent. Hold your personnel accountable but be sure to praise in public and correct in private—unless there is a pressing need such as safety or preventing grave damage to equipment. Lastly, give credit where credit is due—if you have been complimented for something your division has done, be sure to relay those kind words to those most deserving—your Sailors.

Managing Programs

The term "program" is generically used in the Navy to refer to any set of requirements that must be managed and monitored to make sure those requirements are being enforced and maintained. Programs range from ammunition administration to electrical safety with everything in between. Many primary jobs have programs associated with their duties that will naturally fall to you while others will be unrelated to your primary billet and given to you as a collateral duty.

Getting Started

A good place to start the management of your program is to review previous assessments that have been conducted, usually by following a checklist from the Navy instruction that governs your program. By analyzing the previous assessment—particularly if it has been conducted by someone other than your predecessor, such as an outside inspector or subject matter expert—you will be able to focus on the areas of the program that warrant improvement. If your predecessor related these shortcomings and his or her efforts to correct them to you, this is a good sign that the program is "living and breathing." Conversely, if there has been no action taken for some time on shortcomings that have been identified, this is also relevant information.

Some of the biggest building blocks of a program are the publications and instructions that govern it. Some instructions are updated more frequently than others. You will save yourself trouble by making sure your references are up to date.

Success is in the details. If one of your program's requirements is to make sure all equipment is properly bolted down, you will want to make sure that all the right materials are being used for the job. Although you will not be the one bolting down the equipment, confirming that the proper bolts are being used and conducting spot checks to verify the proper installation will be part of your responsibilities.

Documentation

If you are doing all the right things but can't show what you have accomplished, you are setting yourself up for failure. While most assessors are very experienced and will be able to tell if you are managing the program well, most follow the philosophy that "if a requirement wasn't documented, then it hasn't been done." Having a well-organized binder to present your program to an off-ship assessor will not guarantee success, but documenting consistently meeting the program requirements conveys a sense of follow-through that demonstrates you are meeting the objectives of the program.

Whether it is equipment logs, maintenance records, training reports, or counseling chits, make sure you let your shipmates know what documentation you require for your program. If you are not an organized person by nature, you will need to improve in this area since program management is a component of most leadership positions in the Navy. Ask your LCPO and LPO what they have seen work in the past and then work with them to implement it. You should also consider finding someone on your ship who is well regarded for management abilities and take a look at how that person organizes and manages programs.

Managing Assessments and Certifications

Assessments, traditionally referred to as inspections, are a fact of military life. Just as there is a requirement to pass Calculus I before signing up for Calculus II in college, your command will not be able to move forward without passing certain assessments and milestones. Not passing a course may delay graduation for a student, but failing an assessment could mean not being able to deploy on time for a ship or squadron. There can be potential Navy-wide consequences when a ship, submarine, or squadron that failed an assessment is unable to deploy on time.

While not every failed inspection risks delaying a deployment, these setbacks affect morale and your ship's standing, and they often have ramifications on working hours and other quality of life issues. Most Sailors understand that mission comes first. More plainly, no matter how arduous, it is better to prepare well for an assessment once, rather than having to prepare twice for the same assessment after falling short the first time.

Because of the importance of assessments and certifications, the time leading up to an assessment can be stressful. Part of your job will be ensuring that your Sailors understand the broader purpose of the inspection and understand their work schedule and the challenges ahead. If you believe that your Sailors will need to work longer hours than normal or during the weekend, make sure that you discuss this with your department head and chief because many commands require that senior leaders such as the XO or the department head are aware that working hours have been extended.

In the best commands, each program and requirement would get the command-level attention and support it needs to be successful. Due to conflicting requirements, strengths and weaknesses of personnel, and the command's schedule, however, this may not always be the case. As the manager of a given program, one of your roles is to be an advocate for your program and ensure that any training or command involvement required for the program's success is telegraphed effectively.

As you prepare for the upcoming assessment, remember your other duties as well. There is a very human tendency to let noninspection-related items fall by the wayside during the preparations for and execution of an assessment. In today's operational climate, it is not unheard of for commands to be preparing for multiple assessments at the same time—not a surprise for a navy that prides itself on its ability to accomplish multiple missions at once. Through it all, remember to keep your head in the game and your standards high, and to work hard in advance to avoid "cramming" for an assessment at the last minute.

Tactical Preparations

From the supply corps officer who tracks down and procures the parts necessary to keep a jet in the air to the antisubmarine warfare (ASW) officer who serves as the ASW evaluator when her ship is hunting a submarine, almost all of us have tactical roles to play as junior officers. Tactical preparation starts long before any specific event. For aviators, for instance, this training starts at flight school. Each warfare community has warfare-specific publications and manuals as well as tactical memos and case studies. Make it a point to find out what is out there, take the time to read the information you find, and—most importantly—practice the tactical skills and evolutions you will need to demonstrate.

Another way to maintain your situational awareness is to read message traffic, the Navy's system of transmitting plans and policy via radio broadcast. While quite a bit of message traffic is administrative in nature, most tactical information is transmitted via message traffic or via a classified Web site known as the CAS site (collaboration at sea). If there is a training exercise coming up, there will likely be a pre-exercise message that will delineate the specifics for the exercise.

If your CO is the officer conducting the exercise (OCE) or the officer in tactical command (OTC), you may in fact have to draft this message yourself. If your ship or command is taking part in an actual operation, there will be messages that come out in relation to that specific operation's goals and requirements. In addition, the daily intention messages (DIMS) and other warfare-area-specific messages will hold valuable information as well.

You may also be required to attend meetings and briefs that will reinforce what you may have already read as well as let you know of any recent changes to the planned exercise or operation. In some cases you will be required to draft or even deliver a portion of the brief—particularly if there is a tactical evolution associated with your division's principal duties.

If you are responsible for building a tactical brief, take this opportunity seriously by finding briefing templates that work, use the current references, and practice your brief ahead of time in front of your department head to identify any information gaps in your presentation. Even if you are not involved in giving a brief or required to attend the meetings, it is a good idea to attend if you are allowed to do so. You will likely learn quite a bit, and this will contribute significantly to your professional development.

Managing Up

One of the most important relationships you will have is with your immediate superior. There is an old saying that you can manage your boss or your boss will manage you. Rather than take this somewhat adversarial view, think about your working relationship with your boss as a constructive relationship in which you are the junior partner.

"Managing up" in a skillful manner does not imply manipulation or placating your boss through a well-turned phrase. What it does mean is keeping your boss informed of what is going on in your division. If you do this well on a consistent basis, you will demonstrate a command of your organization's requirements that will make your boss much more comfortable with your approach and much less likely to micromanage your efforts.

Your department head will expect quite a bit from you. Expect him or her to ask many questions. At first, you may not know all the answers right off the bat, but you should make it a point to avoid failing to answer the same question twice. Be sure to write down what your boss asks for and to follow up appropriately if you do not initially have an answer ready.

While you are certainly entitled to ask for clarifying guidance, you should not expect your boss to provide all the details for the task at hand. That is your job. Good questions may be related to due date or the format of the desired product (a written report, an e-mail, or a verbal confirmation, for example). If you think there might be a genuine obstacle to completing a task, find time to discuss this more in depth, but avoid the appearance that you are pushing back on a request or attempting to demonstrate how busy you are.

In the beginning, your boss will not be surprised that you have questions. If the deadline permits, it is a good idea to do your own research first and then ask questions. Consider asking a fellow junior officer for additional tips as well. For something within the lifelines of your organization, ask your chief. If you have questions after doing your homework, ask your boss, but do so in an informed manner rather than seeking an answer to a question that you could have researched elsewhere.

One of the key elements of managing up is leaving your boss "room to maneuver" should an unforeseen obstacle occur related to a given task. The best way to do this is to make sure you complete your assignments early or on time. We are all human, and your boss may have things he struggles with. You should pay attention to your boss' strengths and weaknesses and be prepared to adjust to them. Focusing on "what is best for your boss" in relation to meeting a requirement will also help you tailor your methods for success. The bottom line is that when your boss succeeds, so do you.

Managing Collateral Duties

Collateral duties are a part of naval life that you will likely encounter shortly after arriving at your first command. Here are a few of the collateral duties you might be assigned:

★ Legal officer
★ Wardroom mess treasurer

★ Public affairs officer
★ Morale, welfare, and recreation officer or MWR funds custodian
★ Voting assistance officer

Depending on the collateral duty, you may find yourself reporting directly to the XO and CO, or to another senior officer. This may seem stressful at times because of their rank and position, but they will largely have the same needs as the leader to whom you normally report. Simply put, they will want to ensure that the interests of the command are being met by your management of a particular collateral duty.

If you are reporting directly to the CO or XO, it is a good practice to keep your immediate senior informed as well. Just as any collateral duties that your junior personnel own are also your collateral duties to a certain degree, the same goes for your boss. Even though your boss may not have a direct interest in your collateral duty, your time management directly affects a part of the organization's effectiveness. If you keep your boss in the loop, he or she will be able to work with you to balance your other demands, for example, when a program you may be running as a collateral duty is being assessed by experts outside of the command.

Collateral duties can be rewarding. Being able to assist a Sailor gain American citizenship or to register to vote is a very satisfying experience. Collateral duties can also provide an opportunity to distinguish yourself within your command. While your principal focus should always be on your primary duties and operational performance, tackling collateral duties in a positive and focused manner demonstrates that you are ready for more responsibilities in the future.

Planning and Executing

Much of the planning and executing you do will simply be assessing what needs to be done and doing it, but two items can assist with large-scale planning and evaluation. A plan of action and milestones (POA&M) is a widely used tool for planning; there may be one in effect that you can follow, but this is something you can also draft yourself if needed. Checksheets are also an invaluable tool and should be used frequently to assess your programs and areas of responsibility.

Plan of Action and Milestones

A POA&M is a delineation of all requirements related to a comprehensive project; it has a timeline and responsibility assigned for each step required. Frequently centered on an upcoming inspection, deployment, or another complex goal, this document (often a Word or Excel document) provides a clear path to the end goal.

POA&Ms are well-used tools at the vast majority of successful commands. Locate a POA&M that your more experienced peers identify as particularly effective to prepare for a major milestone. You could use this same approach to prepare for significant challenges in your management portfolio as well. Usually broken down in blocks of time before the inspection or deployment (e.g., six months, three months, one month, one week), this document breaks large goals down into more easily managed elements while leaving time to address issues as they come up.

Driving the Checklist

As alluded to earlier in this chapter, checklists, also known as checksheets, are very prevalent in the Navy. Checklists often provide step-by-step guidance for accomplishing a task within specifications. There are also checklists for program management as well as space inspections and divisional requirements (e.g., electrical equipment requirements). Just as you should make sure your publications are up to date before you use them, you should make sure you are using the latest version of checksheets, which are often updated.

Once you obtain the most up-to-date checksheets for your areas of responsibility, read through them yourself. Generally, references are listed at the beginning of the document or are related to each item on the checksheet. These checksheets often offer a "guided tour" through the instructions that dictate the specifics for your program, and it is worth your time to become very familiar with the items on your checksheets.

As you use these documents to evaluate where you stand, the most important thing is to be self-critical. If you are your "own toughest critic," you can often find discrepancies before the assessors do, leaving you time to fix those problems beforehand. If a problem can't be fixed in the short term, it can be documented for a longer-term solution. Finally, when you are done using checksheets to analyze a program or complete an evolution, keep them on file. These checksheets demonstrate consistent program management and will often pinpoint when a problem was identified or fixed.

Ensuring Quality

In a traditional naval division, you may not physically be completing the work that your division is responsible for, but you play a significant role ensuring the quality of your Sailors' work. Your LCPO will be your most valuable partner in this effort, particularly in terms of the technical aspects of your organization's responsibilities.

Administratively, there will be a myriad of reports and documents that you will be required to route through the chain of command. From leave chits to training reports, after your chief looks at the item in question, the chits will be forwarded to you for your review. When reviewing a document—a leave chit, for example—read every single block where information is required. For a training report, for instance, make sure it is in the proper format, that all training requirements for the period of the report are met, and that the supporting documentation required (i.e., muster sheets and critiques) is attached and complete.

Spot checks

The maintenance, material, and management system (3M) is an integral program to our operational fleet. To someone who has never worked with the system before, the initial terms may seem foreign. With effort, you can learn the system that is so important to the incredibly capable Navy that we operate today. Preventive maintenance done correctly prevents unplanned equipment failure. Just as you change the oil in your car every three thousand miles or so to extend its life, preventive maintenance focuses on conducting inspections and servicing and replacing parts with specific life spans to keep equipment operating for longer periods of time.

As a newly commissioned officer, you will likely be required to do maintenance spot checks frequently as a quality check to ensure your personnel are following the guidelines for accomplishing maintenance. Things to keep in mind as you conduct a spot check include the following:

★   Is the person conducting this maintenance properly qualified to do so?
★   Is the correct/most up-to-date procedure being followed?
★   Are the correct tools, lubricants, and parts being used?
★   Is the person following the procedure exactly?
★   Does the person know what safety precautions are applicable to this procedure?

Division in the Spotlight

Your command's Division in the Spotlight (DITS), also referred to in some commands as the command excellence program, is another way to ensure quality across the board for the entire ship or command. While the method and name of this program may vary, most commands in the Navy have some variety of a comprehensive review of a division's or department's readiness. When it is your turn, your DITS inspection will likely include:

★ Zone inspection of the spaces you are responsible for
★ Uniform inspection
★ A 3M spot check with the CO and/or XO
★ Program reviews

Program reviews will be completed by the command's program manager or resident subject matter expert. These reviews will likely be compiled into a single report, presented to the CO, which will create a portrait of the overall health of your division.

Some commands have a schedule that is promulgated ahead of time to allow you to prepare for the review. Other commands conduct a more random selection to promote sustained readiness by not allowing division's times to surge for an inspection, relax, and then surge again when the inspection occurs again. If your predecessor has copies of the last DITS, this will be a very effective tool to get a quick sense of the overall readiness of your division.

Challenges and Rewards Ahead

The wide variety in this chapter points to the many responsibilities you will encounter in your first managerial job as a commissioned officer. Persistence and a positive, steadfast attitude will serve you well as you tackle these challenges. While many tasks will demand that you strive for perfection, there will be some items where you will not want to let "perfect" get in the way of "good." The art of "majoring on the major issues and minoring on the minors" is one that you will develop with time. Remember, you were commissioned because numerous people along the way decided that you have what it takes to be an officer in the world's most powerful Navy—you can do it!

★ 12 ★

GETTING THE MOST OUT OF
NAVAL SCHOOLS

New ensigns will almost invariably attend a naval school in support of their training pipeline to their first assignment. Whether you attend a more comprehensive school such as the naval flight school or a shorter course such as the engagement control officer course for the Tomahawk weapon system, naval schools will play an important role in your professional development.

Although going to school may represent a break in the routine from your primary professional duties at your command, you will want to give these schools your best. For the individual officer, naval schools often represent "free" knowledge, enabling you to gain new skills or improve old ones without the strain of real-world operations or the down side of real-world mistakes that sometimes occur during on-the-job training in an operational setting. But in other ways these courses are anything but free. The Navy is indeed paying for this school, both in terms of the cost it takes to run the course and in terms of time that the course is taking you away from your principal duties.

Of course there are other reasons to take these courses seriously. First, those serving as instructors are often naval leaders who have been handpicked to share their expertise with you based on their own success in the fleet, and it is smart to heed their advice. Second, unlike some of the academic courses you have taken in the past, many of these courses are directly related to a core or collateral duty, so you will want to pay attention because odds are that you will be asked to demonstrate what you have learned in a real-world setting. Third, more naval schools are reporting student performance to parent commands. Most profoundly, your ship and your Sailors will be counting on you to take the lessons you have learned back to your command. This reoccurring theme that your performance no longer affects only you but affects a much larger group of people is one that new naval officers will continually encounter.

HELPFUL HINT—HOW NAVAL SCHOOLS ARE DIFFERENT FROM COLLEGE

Naval schools are a military commitment. Just as for a muster on a ship, do not be late and be prepared to participate in the same way you would be ready for duty or work.

It will not be just you who will be affected by your performance.

Unlike the college experience that you have largely left behind, naval schools help to build your service or business reputation.

Sometimes you cannot take homework home. Because you may be working with classified material, your study may be restricted to certain areas in the naval school compound.

Navy schools often require you to live in temporary lodging for a period of a week to a few months away from your normal place of residence.

Because naval schools may feature activities involving more risk such as small-arms training and live fire-fighting, safety will be stressed much more heavily.

Chain of Command

Just as you will encounter in your first duty station, naval schools also adhere to a chain of command. Your instructors are not only teaching you, but they will likely be your principal leaders as well. They will report up their own chain of command to a department head who in turn reports to the commander of the school. While the actual links in the chain of command will vary, it is important to remember that naval schools will often take a much more holistic approach to student development than the standard civilian institution.

Section Leader

In addition to the assigned staff, many schools customarily assign a member of your class to be the class or section leader, usually based on seniority. The class leader's job usually involves taking attendance and handling basic logistics related to classroom administration. In some cases the section leader will be the first person with whom you discuss any leave or liberty request. As you might imagine, peer leadership can be thankless, so do your best to be supportive and responsive to the section leader. Soon enough you may be a section leader for a naval school and you will appreciate the same treatment from your classmates.

A section leader's responsibilities can be expansive, particularly for naval schools that have lengthier terms, so your section leaders will very likely ask for volunteers to whom they can delegate portions of their responsibilities. These duties could include being a watchbill coordinator for classroom duties such as security, maintaining the coffee mess, or arranging a class event at graduation. While the lesser side of human nature might make you inclined to avoid pitching in, do your best to find an area to help. By pitching in, you are doing the right thing, and in many cases these relationships with your school classmates contribute to your fleet reputation over time.

Staff Mentors

In larger courses, a more senior officer and member of the staff may be assigned as your class leader or mentor. These officers (or senior enlisted leaders) are valuable resources during the course and can often help you to prepare better for the course and to take care of personnel challenges that you have.

In some cases, staff mentors may fulfill many of the duties that a section leader might otherwise fill, and student section leaders often directly interface with the staff mentor. Once again, your best approach will be to positively comply with the direction the staff mentor gives and be a good teammate by pitching in on whatever project or task may be required to support the class. If these leaders are senior commissioned officers, you will also want to ensure that you are giving them the respect that their rank and position warrants; even though you may be sitting in the classroom, they deserve the same respect that you afford senior officers in the fleet.

Commanders of the Schools

Most schools, even those with short courses, will be part of a broader array of courses that comprise a naval school command. For schools with longer courses, the commander of the naval school command may visit your class. Just like the dean of a civilian college, these leaders have had successful careers—not in the field of academics but in the fleet. With this in mind, be sure to be respectful of these leaders if you encounter them, but also realize that in many school cultures, students rarely interact with the commander of the school.

Instructors

Instructors are the lifeblood of naval schools. These subject-matter experts will often be senior in rank to you, but they may be experienced senior and junior enlisted. While they will respect your rank, they will have positional authority over you in your class and are charged with your education and your safety, so give them the respect they deserve.

Learning Smarter, Not Harder

For most of us, some previous academic experience has taught us to follow basic studying fundamentals to succeed. For a lucky few, your natural

Not all Navy schools take place in the classroom. Members of a BUD/S class participate in the intensive physical training that is one of the hallmarks of the SEAL community. (U.S. Navy, PH2 Eric Logsdon)

talent and intelligence may have allowed you to succeed in previous academic environments without following an organized study regimen. In
many naval schools, however, time will be short and the academic material
may be new, so it is best to follow good academic practices. Even if you
are confident, remember that your performance in your naval course will
not be important just to you but also to the men and women who will be
counting on you in the fleet.

Cooperate to Graduate
Because the Navy is a "team sport," many of its schools reflect this spirit
of teamwork and encourage collaboration through group projects and
study groups. As always, make sure that you understand what policies exist
regarding collaboration—as efficient as a group effort may be, you never
want to sacrifice your integrity to merely improve performance in a naval
school. If the school's policies do allow for student cooperation (and keeping in mind that you will still have to take the exams yourself), you can
often improve your learning through study groups.

Participate in an Outline Exchange
In longer classes, it can really help to have each class member compose an
outline of a given lecture or assigned reading and share that with members
of a study group, or perhaps the whole class. Once again, ensure this is

legal and do not skip reading the assigned material merely because you have someone else's outline. Instead, use the outlines to complement your own preparation and keep these on hand for exams because they can serve as very helpful guides when you are reviewing several subject areas for a test. Beware of older outlines that have been passed down from previous editions of the course you are in; information often changes as practices and procedures evolve in the Navy.

Read the Syllabus
Almost every naval course has a syllabus for its class. Very similar to what you have seen in college, this document will tell you who is teaching the course, what the readings will be, the topic, and other related requirements to the course. Take some time to review this and be sure to retain it during the course as well as after you return to the ship. These guides will enable you to best prepare for the lesson and will often allow you to identify who the subject-matter expert is for a given area if you have problems.

Find Your Best Place to Study
Just as you have experienced in high school and college, the quality of your study time can be hugely dependent on where you study. Be realistic about your powers of concentration and your ability to avoid distractions at home, and pick the place where you can most effectively and efficiently prepare.

Read the Assignment before Class
Because some of the concepts in a naval course may be fairly specialized and new, it will help you to read the assigned course material before the instructor discusses it. This may seem like common sense, but many students in and out of the military make the mistake of counting on the instructor to teach them the material while they receive the information passively without preparing for the lesson. You will learn much more effectively by reading the material beforehand.

Go to the Review Sessions
The form and content of course material review sessions can vary, but in many cases the instructor will focus on the concepts he or she thinks are important, and these concepts will likely appear on the test. These review sessions often occur outside of normal class time and are voluntary, but they are almost always worth attending. If this is a longer course with several tests scheduled, attending the first review will also give you a good sense of how reliable the reviews are for future tests.

Seek Out Extra Practice or Instruction if You Need It

While some naval courses are more theoretical, most are oriented to equip you with a particular experience or skill. The faculty will certainly be interested in helping you to develop that skill, but you will often be the best judge of how you are progressing.

Just like life, some students will have a prior background or innate aptitude that allows them to pick up a specific skill more quickly than others. If you are not that type of person, look for additional opportunities to practice the skills that are being taught. Everyone wants to do well in front of his or her peers; just remember that making mistakes in the classroom—and learning from them—will allow you to move past those obstacles when you are expected to perform those duties in the fleet.

What if You Already Know the Subject Matter of the Course Well?

Because some naval courses are requirements for every command in the Navy, you may wind up in a course that touches on a subject matter area where you already have a great deal of experience. If this is the case, be courteous to the instructor and your class by serving as a helpful asset in the class rather than reminding everyone how smart you are.

The Navy is constantly reviewing its course subjects, so several things might have changed since you last took the course or were trained in an area. In the last decade, for example, there have been a number of changes to the main space fire doctrine (MSFD) that ships use to combat fires, changes a student might not be aware of if they had last concentrated on this area some time ago.

If you are attending a naval course that covers familiar material, use this as a chance to enhance or reaffirm your knowledge. Even if the course is a complete repeat for you, remember that getting a chance to build "your muscle memory" in an activity your command is counting on you to master never hurts.

Preparing before the Course

Work with your command's school coordinators to find out what the prerequisites are for a given naval course. For some courses, such as the Visit Board Search and Seizure (VBSS) School that is required for boarding team members on surface ships, the prerequisites are comprehensive enough to include physical, medical, and training requirements that will compel your command to have a whole program in place to ensure that you are eligible and prepared for the training. The prerequisites and requirements are not that extensive for most courses, but you will want to use a little advance planning to make sure that you are as prepared as possible for your course.

If the course you are attending is fairly common, check with more experienced junior officers to see if they attended and if they have any material from the course. Be sure to talk to them about their experiences, and explicitly ask them what they wish they knew about the course before starting it. Scanning or quickly reading any materials they have retained will give you a better sense of comfort as you begin the course of instruction. Finally, if you live in the town where the school is located or arrive there a day or two early, take a dry run to the class location the day before class. This will cut down on the chances of a stressful first morning and prevent you from being late on the first day of class.

Being late to class on the first day of any school is never a good feeling, but in some naval courses being late may mean that you could lose your spot (more formerly referred to as a "quota") in class. Many naval courses are so sought after that commands will send potential students to the first day of class on "standby," in hopes of replacing a student who has failed to show for class. In addition to being on time, make sure that you arrive in the correct uniform as well.

After the Course

Make sure that you keep your notes if this is permitted. Although class notes will not substitute for reviewing the reference that guides a given subject area, saving this material will give you a great ready reference of the material for the future. Because most naval schools are focused on a topic or skill set you will rely on to perform your job, you will find yourself returning to previous course material much more often than you likely did in college. Remember that course material and lesson guides can become obsolete, so always ensure that you are reviewing naval references as well.

If the course offers computer CDs or printed material, be sure to take those as well. This material will often play a role in a qualification board if it is related to the core competencies of your specific service community. Be a good shipmate and let your department head and peers know that you have this material to share. This will ensure that the next person from your command will also be well prepared. Finally, many naval school commands and instructors will provide you contact information so that you can contact them if you have a question once you have left the course. There have been a number of instances in the fleet where being able to reach back to the instructors of a previous course can clarify a question that is critical to your command's performance during an inspection or an exercise in the fleet.

Other Considerations Unique to the Naval Classroom.

Naval schools can be very different from traditional academic experiences, so there are other aspects of naval coursework to consider as well.

Administration

Every naval course you attend will require orders. These may be as simple as one-page no-cost orders to attend a school near your parent command or one of many intermediate stops included in a longer set of orders associated with a permanent change of duty station. You will need to ensure that these orders are "endorsed" by the school's administrative staff. Your orders will likely be required to enable you to stay at a combined bachelor quarters near the school you are attending. If you are away from your permanent command, make sure that you retain your lodging receipts and travel receipts to support filing a travel claim to recoup your expenses after the course.

Security

Throughout your naval career, you will be entrusted with sensitive material; the material at naval schools is no exception. The Navy's more comprehensive tactical schools often have quite a bit of classified material being handled by students, so do not be surprised to see extra safeguards in place. For instance, you may have to periodically serve as the student who secures the classroom in the evening, ensuring that classified safes are locked at the end of the academic day. Naval schools have programs in place to inform their students of the classification of the course material and how that material should be handled, but if you have any doubts, ask your instructor for guidance.

Course Critiques

The Navy prides itself on continually focusing on improvement, so in the vast majority of naval schools, you will be asked to provide feedback on a given course. Just as you might expect, this should not be taken as an opportunity to settle old scores or take a free shot at a tough instructor, but you will definitely be encouraged to provide feedback. Not surprisingly, being constructive in your criticism is the best strategy.

No one likes to come up short in the eyes of a student, and most instructors want to get better and want to more effectively pass on their knowledge to students. Concentrating on areas that you found particularly helpful as well as areas you wish were more comprehensively covered are usually helpful approaches. If you observe a shortcoming or behavior that is truly troubling early in the class, do not wait to share this information in the course critique at the end of the course—seek out your section leader or instructors right away.

Leave and Liberty
Since naval schools represent an investment in you and an opportunity cost in terms of others not attending, taking leave or liberty during normal workdays will be discouraged (holidays and winter breaks are the usual exceptions). If there is a compelling personal need that you believe may necessitate leave (the birth of a child for example), be sure to discuss this with your section leader and staff mentor as soon as you sense this situation may emerge. Just as with the fleet, sharing your challenges with your school chain of command in a timely manner gives them the greatest opportunity to help you.

Standing Watch
If the course is particularly long or is housed at its own facility, you may be assigned some watches or required to stand duty for a day. These are usually small or infrequent responsibilities, but perform them to the best of your ability. Once again, people appreciate a team player.

Beyond the Classroom
Get to Know Your Classmates
Some lifelong friendships have started in a naval classroom. Like any activity in life, it is best to have friends who share these common experiences, so look to make a connection with those students who share the classroom with you. Besides the human dimension, you will be surprised how much you can learn from officers from other commands. Over time these relationships can prove helpful and can give you a person outside of the lifelines of your command when you are looking for advice or merely want to know what it is like in another command in the Navy.

Get to Know Your Instructors
Although your instructors are placed at the head of a class to do a job, get to know them as well. If they are senior officers or enlisted leaders, it would be inappropriate to pursue a peer relationship with them, but instructors have at times become lifelong mentors for their past students. Additionally, most instructors have been detailed to their positions based on their career success and subject matter knowledge. While you will always want to be authentic and respect the time of the faculty, making a small connection with them and staying in touch afterward might prove beneficial down the road if you have a question or issue after you leave the course.

Live Close to the Schoolhouse

If the school is a long one, pick a place to live that is "close to the school-house." While many training schools outside of your home port will strongly encourage or require you to live in a CBQ (combined bachelor's quarters), some longer schools will be classified as a permanent change of station and you will be afforded an opportunity to pick where you are going to live.

Living more than thirty minutes away from where the course is taught will affect your quality of life—particularly if you have to make two round trips to support night study. The vast majority of naval courses will commence and conclude during the heart of rush hour, so be sure to ask about rush hour commute times (and better yet test them yourself) before committing to a great place that is farther away from your school.

The longer the course, the more likely night study may be involved to appropriately prepare for the exams. If your course is tactically oriented, some of your course material will be classified, which will almost make it a certainty that you will have to return to the classroom at night to study at times.

Attending a Naval School in the Same Area as Your Command

If your school is short and in the area of your command, make it a practice to return to your command after school unless your boss tells you differently. This may not be feasible for some of the more demanding courses, but doing this will ease your burden when you complete your coursework and will signal to your chain of command that you have not lost sight of your core responsibilities.

Returning to your command at the end of a school day is not always easy, and many young officers have observed that schools outside of your home port area tend to be easier to manage, but in the long run, returning to your command is a sound practice. A quick visit that allows you to briefly scan your naval e-mail account, touch base with your chief on the week ahead, and scan your in-box for any new assignments will help prevent you from feeling overwhelmed or badly surprised when you return after completing your school. Even if it is impossible to come back every day, periodically visiting your parent command will make things much easier for you when you return to your primary duties.

Watch Your Conduct

Although you may feel far away from your home command while you are attending a naval course, in some ways you are never closer. When you are at school, you are a representative of your command. Many commanding officers have received a complimentary phone call—or a negative one—that has helped to establish a young officer's trajectory in a new command. So in addition to being a good steward for your command while you are in the classroom, be mindful of your conduct outside of it.

As you should at all times, avoid alcohol-related misconduct, particularly driving while under the influence of alcohol. This violation, as well as other legal interactions with the police, will inevitably make their way back to your parent command. Simply put, make sure you are making responsible choices in both your academic and social life.

Get a Workout and Get Your Sleep
Unlike the high activity, interactions with people, and the adrenaline of shared efforts and deadlines that often keep your job vibrant during the day in your normal work environment, academic settings will usually demand that you have better rest. Most of us have struggled with the tough experience of concentrating more on staying awake than on the course material at hand—do not let this happen to you.

For officers attending a course and returning to their command each night, managing rest can be especially tricky. Particularly if you are in a duty section, you may be asked to stand a watch when you return to your duty day following the school day. Although this will likely only happen every few days, do everything you can to work with your duty section leader to avoid going to school with only three to four hours of rest.

In addition to being well rested for your course, you should also keep up with physical conditioning. For a shorter class, this will help you stay alert in class. For longer courses, particularly those where you are living away from your parent command, you will want to stay fit and avoid returning to your command having gained a few pounds—an easy trap to fall into if you are eating out more frequently while you are away from home.

Have Fun
If you are attending a naval course outside of your home port that lasts more than a week, look for some activities on the weekend beyond watching television in a hotel room or going to the closest bar. All naval bases have a morale, welfare, and recreation (MWR) representative who can help you with identifying attractions in the area, sporting events, or even day trips that you would enjoy. Although there is certainly nothing wrong with grabbing a drink with friends or watching a ball game on television, look to enhance your experiences as you progress through your career by more fully exploring the areas you are assigned to—one of the genuinely fun aspects of naval life.

Leading and Learning: A Way of Life

Naval schools are one of the great components of the Navy's commitment to lifelong learning while you serve. Few professions invest as heavily in continued education, and as a newly commissioned officer, your commitment to these courses should be nothing but your best. Your command, your shipmates, and your Sailors deserve nothing less, and the lessons you learn in the classroom may save lives in the fleet during times of trial.

★ 13 ★

VOICES OF COMMAND

Although leadership abounds at all levels in a successful chain of command, no one sets the tone for the command more than the commanding officer. As you begin your first few months as an ensign, your interaction with your captain may range from daily interaction at a small operational command to much less frequent contact in some larger commands. Even with the best commanding officers, the demands on their time may preclude them from providing you direct advice and counsel on what a brand-new ensign can do to succeed. In this chapter, several distinguished commanding officers from a variety of service communities directly pass on their advice to you.

Time Management: The Universal Challenge

Before I move on to the subject at hand, I must first congratulate those of you who are reading this as you prepare to report to your first ship. What you have chosen to do is extraordinary; serving one's country is an act of great selflessness, and as a newly retired officer, I am grateful to every young man or woman who chooses to serve this great nation, especially in the U.S. Navy.

You are about to undertake a life quite unlike the one you left behind, irrespective of your commissioning source. For those of you joining the fleet from Annapolis, you will now take for granted time and freedom that were doled out to you previously as privileges. For those of you joining the fleet from NROTC, you will get used to a whole new level of structure and rigor in your once carefree lives. For those of you joining your first wardroom from the enlisted ranks, you will be exposed to a far different professional atmosphere than the one you left on the mess decks or the CPO mess, one that places demands on you that you did not previously have.

The one thing that ties all of these experiences together is the absolute necessity to manage your own time. Nothing you have done thus far has prepared you for the incredible demands that will soon be placed on your

The commanding officer not only leads his command tactically but is also the most senior mentor on the ship. (U.S. Navy, SN Jessica Pounds)

time. Thrust out into the working world now with some money in your pocket to enjoy the finer things in life, you will arrive at the ship often before the sun rises and just as often leave after the sun sets. You will have to spend time learning how to be a good leader and manager (and you must be both), tracking down repairs, and seeing to the development of your people, even as you are faced with a grueling and often relentless need to develop your own professional skills. You will have demands placed on your time by your friends, family, and spouse or significant other. Oh, and by the way, you will need to spend time tending to your own physical fitness to stay within standards.

What I am describing is a witch's brew of conditions that can and will cause you to believe that there are not enough hours in the day to do all the things you need to do. Without developing a solid set of skills and tools designed to manage your time effectively, you will quickly get behind the power curve, a curve that some simply never transcend. To provide a bit of insight into what some of those tools might be, I humbly offer the following, and I hope one or more of these tools might be of use to you.

★ Goals are for chumps; plans are for winners. Everyone has goals; winners actually achieve them. Achieving goals is a function of the dedicated application of time and energy to a set of preplanned milestones chronologically ordered in a manner designed to achieve the objective. Write down your plans. Share them with your boss; ask his or her opinion on how logical or achievable your plan is. Work with your chief to devise plans. Constantly update your plans. Don't make a plan and then set it on the shelf, and don't make a plan that you are unwilling to alter. Make your subordinates plan, and make them show you their plans. Effective planning is one of the most effective ways to conserve your most precious asset: your time.

★ Guard your personal time jealously and use it effectively. The Navy expects you to maintain physical fitness standards, so carve out time to work out (and no, not only on YOUR time). During the course of the workday, carve out time where you can work on your priorities without interruption. Of course, your boss or the CO or XO can interrupt, but tell your chief that you really need this time. Use it to plan, use it for your own professional development, use it to read and answer your e-mail. But be ruthless in protecting it, and that means protecting it from the newfound (and less disciplined) friends you will meet in the wardroom.

★ Make time to be social. One of the very best things about wardroom life is the social aspect, replicated almost nowhere else, certainly not in the corporate world. Be open to social events with your shipmates. Hang out with each other, help each other navigate the world that each of you inhabits. Everything in moderation, including fun. Going to sea is too hard a life for there not to be a good bit of fun bound up in it. Enjoy it.

★ Before you leave the ship each day, take the next day's plan of the day (POD) and use it to plan out your day, including personal time. Discuss this personal plan the next day with your divisional leadership so they know what your priorities are. It is much easier to get blown from one thing to another when you don't have a plan.

The emphasis I place on time management is not something I came by late in my career. I was lucky enough to have people early on tell me how important it would be, and by the time I was fortunate enough to command my own destroyer, I taught and mentored a generation of officers in how to be more effective. I wish each of you great good luck, and I urge you to quickly discover how best to manage your own time. It will make all the difference.

CDR Bryan McGrath retired in 2008. He commanded USS *Bulkeley* (DDG 84) from 2004–6, during which the ship earned the USS *Arizona* Memorial Trophy and the Battle Efficiency "E," and he earned the Surface Navy Association's Zumwalt Award for Inspirational Leadership.

Professional Expertise, Attitude, Initiative

Any time an O-6 attempts to communicate with a junior officer, there is well-known statistical evidence that documents the tendency of the JO to ignore the "older" generation. The perception is that there is no way that the analog old man can possibly understand the current plight of the digital, high-speed JO. I'm old enough to be your father, and I admit that my eight-year-old child can consistently kick my butt with a Nintendo, X-box, or Wii. In relation to you, I am as old as dirt, but to keep it in perspective, after twenty-four years of dedicating my life to the Navy, the Navy has become as much of a family as my own bloodline, and I offer my "fatherly" advice to you with the same love and admiration that I would offer guidance to my own sons and daughters.

There are three primary qualities that have consistently proven to help JOs rise to the top, but they do not include sucking up to your superiors. First, you must become dependably competent at your warfare profession. If you are an aviator, know your naval air training and operating procedures standards (NATOPS) and emergency procedures better than your peers, and be so good at flying, or navigating, or weaponeering, that developing situational awareness inside the cockpit is the only challenge that remains. We in the prehistoric generation have all been JOs, and we have tremendous respect for young men and women who pursue perfection in the careers to which we have already dedicated our lives and the lives of our families. We know firsthand that it is not an easy task, so we admire JOs who follow in our footsteps to develop their talents in such a noble profession. If you also show a genuine desire to improve, most good leaders will help you until their dying breath. Admittedly, some of you will wish for that last breath to hit your CO before your tour is over, but just remember that although the "help" may come at times in the form of a verbal reprimand that might scorch your eyebrows off (appropriate, at times, depending on the severity of the situation), we have all made many of the same mistakes that you will make, but we honestly want you to succeed. A senior naval officer's only true legacy is the junior officers that learn from him or her.

Let's talk more about "naval officer attitude"—or what I believe is truly the golden nugget. You cannot get it in a NATOPS book and you cannot buy it (as Richard Gere bought his spit-shined boots in the movie *An Officer and a Gentleman*). This quality comes from within. This attitude includes a burning desire to become a better professional naval officer—a realization that serving your country is a duty much larger than yourself or your individual talents. It is an awakening that you are proud to wear the same uniform as did the many heroic men and women who have given their lives in service to our great nation to preserve the American values of freedom and justice. You cannot fake it. It has to be genuine. There are those of you who will understand this attitude before your peers, and it will become the catalyst for you to excel. It will be the reason that you stay longer hours to get a quality product turned out. It will be the reason that it makes sense to you to deploy, leaving friends and family at home, making less money than your civilian college buddies at home in their houses. This attitude might even manifest itself in a couple pizzas that you buy out of your own pocket to show your night-shift Sailors how much you appreciate their hard work through the mid shift.

Finally, the third quality that immediately makes a JO shine is the genuine appreciation of the calling to serve your country. This is a wealth of inspiration and self-motivation that will be the sustaining drive that distinguishes you as an outstanding junior officer. This personal drive and initiative is critical to your success. Be the junior officer that is inspired to volunteer. Volunteer your time and effort for all tasks, those assigned or assumed. Be the JO who finds something that can be improved upon and does it without being told to do it. I have been especially appreciative of the JOs who have identified a problem area and then proposed their ideas for personally helping resolve it. Believe me, if senior officers had more time on our hands, we would be finding the same problems and trying to get them fixed—we have made a successful career out doing of this—so your personal initiative will be appreciated and hopefully will be rewarded.

Well, I have waxed relatively poetical for a guy who was told as an ensign by two Field Naval Aviator Evaluation Boards that he should pursue another career. But I never gave up, and I'm still here to write this letter to my replacements today. We have discussed professional expertise, attitude, and initiative—three qualities that have been invaluable to me and any of the junior officers whom I have had the pleasure of serving with and serving for. As a parting word of advice from this "dear old dad," know that you will serve many leaders in your naval career, some good and, honestly, some just plain bad. I encourage each of you to evaluate the qualities that you respect in the inspirational leaders and note the qualities you never want to replicate in the others. And for God's sake, do not let the relatively short duration that you may serve a bad leader affect your decision to proudly serve our country. That knucklehead will not continue to be a leader in our Navy, and you will grow to be a better leader to take his or her place. Remember, a majority of your personal naval legacy—the young men and women whom you will mold and mentor—are in all likelihood yet to be born. This is a commitment for the long run, to be sure, but a long run most assuredly worth taking.

Brian Hinckley was the first commander, Joint CREW Composite Squadron ONE (JCCS-1), Baghdad, Iraq, neutralizing the RC-IED threat in Operation Iraqi Freedom, and previously had command at sea of VAQ-135, deployed in combat operations for Operation Enduring Freedom and Operation Iraqi Freedom.

Managing Relationships, Maturity, Passion, and Trust

My first meetings with new officers of a sea-air-land (SEAL) team are in equal measure discussing my expectations of them as well as determining their strengths, weaknesses, interests, and special skills to slot them into a platoon or other job at the team. How does each person fit into the team beyond whatever billet is to be filled? Platoon officers often weigh personality matters quite heavily because the relationship between the two officers in a platoon, chief and LPO, goes a long way in making a platoon better or worse than the sum of its parts. In this vein I ask a lot of questions about the reporting officer's background, education, unique personal experiences, language skills, and training experience. In the last instance, I also want to know with whom they went through training, both officer and enlisted, because it is sometimes necessary to break up classmates into different platoons.

Intertwined throughout this process of getting to know the new officer and mentally slotting him within the command, I discuss my expectations. I concentrate on three things. I start with what traditionally can be a real issue for new officers in the SEAL teams: trying to be one of the boys. New officers may have gone through training with them and know them quite well, but their relationships must now evolve. This can mean different things to different officers. Some understand and are already living the concept; others require additional counseling by the XO, platoon chief, or platoon commander. In rare cases, officers are at the opposite extreme and are too aloof. This problem is actually far more difficult to address and one that a new officer usually does not outgrow with time at the command. This problem is rare, and there is a large range between being overly aloof and overly familiar in which to develop a suitable leadership style. The majority of officers ultimately find their personal style; some just need to be guided and reminded where it is.

I next focus on a broad area I label maturity. I discuss many things here, but it can be best summed up as understanding what the role of an officer in the SEAL teams is and realizing that it is much more than pure operational prowess. SEAL officers should be strong operators, but they also need to be strong leaders. Moral courage, personal responsibility, and self-discipline are all aspects of this leadership. The basic underwater demolition team/SEAL (BUD/S) mentality of "if you're not cheating, you're not trying" has to now be tempered with the realization that their actions could have serious consequences for themselves and others.

Finally, and tied closely to the notion of leadership, is what I term passion. I want the members of my command to be passionate about what they are doing. They need to master the skills of the trade, not just learn them or be exposed to them. This is hard because there is a lot of ground to cover, but I ask them to be the best they can be and supplement their training with professional reading. I believe that new officers should read not just about SEAL operations but also about a diverse range of subjects because you never know what might turn out to be helpful. I also encourage them to work on their skills as communicators because—whether giving an operational brief or writing an evaluation—communication skills are essential to being a leader. These skills make for successful missions and get their personnel promoted and recognized.

From this initial guidance, I continue to assess these officers and watch how they develop through training and gaining experience. As our predeployment training nears its end, I begin to assess the most important thing of all: my combined rational and intuitive assessment that an officer has my full trust and confidence to lead SEALs and other assigned personnel in combat. This is more than just the sum of operational skill and leadership. The element of trust enters into it. I have had great leaders and operators, but without this trust and confidence it is all for naught.

For me, trust is built on a continuing relationship with an officer where periodically I see that the leader does what is right in a variety of situations. He does not have to always do what is absolutely right, but what he thinks is right at the time, given the information at hand. This is a lot higher bar than it seems, and not everyone can get over that bar. But as we prepared to deploy some platoons to Iraq, this trust in an officer's judgment and confidence in his skills was essential.

Given the opportunity to command again, I would stress that what I look for is an officer who continuously and passionately works to develop and refine his skills as a leader and operator while doing what is right, given the information he has at the time.

CAPT Alex Krongard, a graduate of Princeton University and the National War College, commanded Seal Team 7 during a deployment in Iraq for which he earned the Bronze Star.

Motivation, Intellect, and Example

When a capable officer has the deck, the discipline and safety of the ship are intact. Conversely, when a deficient officer has the deck, discipline breaks down and safety is compromised; the ship might not run afoul, but its reliability will be that of a drifting wreck.

Your service as a commissioned officer in a warship places you at the nexus of people and mission, where responsibility peaks and accountability is absolute. The first precept of a division officer is to learn and understand the standing orders, battle orders, and commander's intent. Command of a warship is not a reward doled out to those in good favor or for time served; the privilege of command is recognition of professional mastery. A warship relies on the knowledge, experience, and judgment of its captain. The captain is responsible and accountable for the safety of the ship and the performance and discipline of the crew. As a division officer, you fill an important leadership role in the ship.

The operating environment of a warship at sea is chaotic. Your obligation is to ensure that the captain's knowledge, experience, and judgment as articulated through orders and intent bear on all situations. The captain expects you, as a leader, to act on your training, of your own initiative, in accordance with commander's intent, and in compliance with the standing and battle orders. During an officer of the deck qualification board a young officer was asked, "Why should the captain qualify you as officer of the deck?" The young officer replied, "Because the captain cannot be on the bridge twenty-four hours a day. As the officer of the deck, I act by, with, and through the captain to serve as his eyes, ears, and voice." I doubt there is a more complete answer or expression of the trust, faith, and confidence demanded by a captain of the officer of the deck.

A warship is not judged by the awards it receives but by the performance of its crew in the preparation and execution of combat operations. Excellence in engineering, seamanship, navigation, communication, war fighting, and damage control, to name a few, represent the "Float—Move—Communicate—Fight" ethos that translates combat readiness into action. Training and disciplined execution ensure a warship's combat readiness and are fundamental to operational success and mission accomplishment. In my mind, validated by my own experiences in command, if a warship lacks the fundamentals, nothing else will sustain it when challenged. As a division officer, you will be called upon to execute the tactics, techniques, and procedures outlined in the ship's doctrine. To do so effectively, you must possess the discipline to act without prompting to accomplish assigned tasks. In short, combat readiness is the foundation for success in all shipboard operations, in peacetime and war, and disciplined execution is its hallmark.

The greatest asset of a warship is the talent, energy, and dedication of its Sailors—your shipmates. In this regard, the importance of your individual leadership cannot be overstated. There are tremendous reservoirs of untapped potential within each of your shipmates waiting to be tapped by a capable leader. As a leader, your task is to evoke the highest individual performance from each member of your team. Evoking high individual performance starts with setting the conditions for growth, learning, and teamwork. It requires you to identify the values the surface warfare community seeks to cultivate, nurture, and sustain from one generation to the next. Among these values are duty, honor, mission, and integrity. Remember, followers confer leadership. As a division officer, you will be given subordinates; as a leader, you will have to earn followers.

Your efforts will at times be greeted by disinterest and reluctance from seniors, peers, and subordinates. You must demand that your shipmates act boldly in action and deed, and insist on doing right without concern for personal consequence. The tools at your disposal are numerous. I recommend you start by focusing on three: motivation, intellect, and example. I value motivation in an officer more than any quality except judgment. Motivation will lead you early in your naval career to take charge of your own professional development. The power of your intellect will yield well-reasoned decisions that demonstrate sound judgment. Finally, the power of your example will focus the efforts of your division and guide each member to act in a manner that will always honor those for whom we serve—country, shipmates, family, and self.

Aristotle once said, "We are what we repeatedly do; excellence, then, is not an act but a habit." Whether standing watch on the bridge, in the central control station, at your console in the combat information center, or with boots on the deck of a ship you have just boarded; whether on duty, leave, or liberty, making excellence a habit is the truest path to success. This can only happen with clear understanding of the captain's orders; intent, steadfast commitment to disciplined execution; and utmost respect for the covenant of trust, faith, and confidence shared between the captain and the officer.

I am proud of your decision to become a surface warfare officer. The work ahead is not easy—at times, it will be frustrating and tough. I am convinced that by being the kind of leader from whom your shipmates can draw strength and inspiration, you can have a positive impact on your ship. After all, it is the impact you have on others, not the impact others have on you, that provides the greatest professional satisfaction. Ultimately, the respect and admiration reflected in the eyes of your shipmates are reward enough for your service, sacrifice, and commitment. I wish you fair winds and following seas.

CDR Vincent D. McBeth completed tours in seven warships, including command of USS *McCampbell* (DDG 85) and USS *Tempest* (PC 2). Ashore, he served as administrative aide to the Secretary of the Navy, White House Fellow to the President, and special assistant to the Chairman of the Joint Chiefs of Staff and the Chief of Naval Operations. He holds a B.S. from the U.S. Naval Academy, an M.A. from The Fletcher School, and an M.S. from the National War College.

Appendix 1
Overview of the History of the U.S. Navy

The humble beginnings of what was to become the greatest Navy in history began with George Washington, who commissioned two armed vessels at his own expense in the fall of 1775 to intercept British supply ships approaching the rebellious North American colonies. On 13 October, the Continental Congress officially sanctioned Washington's actions and the Continental Navy was born.

By 1779, the overmatched Continental Navy had been all but swept from the seas by the mighty Royal Navy, but American privateers—privately funded and operating under official sanction from Congress—captured hundreds of British merchant ships, providing valuable war supplies to the colonies and driving up the cost of shipping in Britain. This strategy of *guerre de course*, or war against commerce, would be returned to again and again over the next two centuries. John Paul Jones—the most acclaimed naval figure of the war—fought his most famous battle off the English coast while attacking a British convoy of merchant ships, defeating the HMS *Serapis* in the old converted merchant ship *Bonhomme Richard*. Uttering the battle cry "I have not yet begun to fight!" while his ship was sinking beneath his feet, he battered the superior *Serapis* into submission and sailed her in triumph to France.

George Washington, reflecting on the war, wrote, "It follows then, as sure as night succeeds the day, that without a decisive naval force we can do nothing definitive—and with it, everything honorable and glorious." Despite General Washington's opinion, following the American victory at Yorktown, the remaining units of the fleet were sold off and the Navy ceased to exist in 1785. Without a navy to defend American interests, merchant ships all over the world came under attack, particularly in Mediterranean waters where the small kingdoms of the Barbary Coast had long preyed on passing vessels.

Recognizing the pressing need for a respectable navy, on 7 March 1794 Congress passed a bill authorizing the construction of six frigates. These vessels, including the immortal *Constitution*, were among the fastest and most powerful sailing frigates ever built, an early example of the long tradition of American technical prowess and innovation at sea. President Jefferson sent a four-ship squadron to the Mediterranean—the beginnings of another long naval tradition of overseas presence. The war with the

Barbary Pirates that followed produced some of America's greatest naval heroes—names that grace the sterns of warships today: Preble, Bainbridge, Truxtun, and the indomitable Decatur.

The United States and Great Britain began a slide toward war again in 1807 when HMS *Leopard* attacked USS *Chesapeake* in her namesake body of water over the issue of naturalized American citizens who had emigrated (the British would say "deserted") from Britain. *Leopard* fired four broadsides into *Chesapeake* and seized four sailors, provoking nationwide outrage. In the first year of the War of 1812, American warships won a series of brilliant single-ship actions against the battle-hardened Royal Navy while USS *Essex*, under CAPT David Porter, ran wild in the Pacific and Indian Oceans, seizing British whalers and disrupting trade. In the American interior, Oliver Hazard Perry scratched together a fleet that swept the British from the great lakes at the battle of Lake Erie (after the battle he tersely wrote, "We have met the enemy, and he is ours"), while Thomas Macdonough's action on Lake Champlain was a decisive American victory that prevented a British advance out of Canada. The war sputtered to a halt in 1815 with the Treaty of Ghent.

Blockade, Brown Water, and the Birth of Modern Naval Warfare

During the Civil War from 1861 to 1865, the great preponderance of naval officers remained with the Union—less than one-fifth of serving naval personnel in 1861 resigned to join the Confederacy (the greatest naval hero of the war, Union admiral David Farragut, was born in Alabama). Within days of the shelling of Fort Sumter, a war against commerce began as the North attempted to strangle the Confederacy with a blockade while the South attempted to disrupt Union commerce at sea and run supplies through the Union-imposed blockade in the South.

The Civil War was also the incubator of the modern U.S. Navy—indeed, of all modern naval warfare. Steam propulsion, armor, turreted guns, mines, and the submarine all emerged during this conflict. From an operational point of view, amphibious warfare, joint operations with the army, and the application of industrial age production were also all brought to the fore.

This technical revolution was on display when USS *Monitor* and CSS *Virginia* (more popularly known by her former Union name of *Merrimack*) met in March 1862—the world's first battle between steam-powered ironclad ships. This battle on the water of Hampton Roads, while inconclusive, previewed the future of naval warfare. In another first, in 1864 a successful submarine attack was carried out by CSS *Hunley*, sinking USS *Husatonic* in Charleston harbor (and incidentally sinking herself for the fourth time in the process).

The Union Navy, in cooperation with the Army, seized the South's major ports, one by one. In August 1864 Admiral Farragut attacked Mobile, Alabama. Hanging off the rigging of his flagship *Harford*, in the midst of close-quarters battle, he ordered her to slew around the ship ahead with a cry of "Damn the torpedoes! Full speed ahead!" ("torpedo" was the early name for a mine). Mobile Bay was taken, and the last major port in the South was closed to the Confederacy. Later that year, ADM David Porter, son of the man who commanded *Essex* during the War of 1812, and his forces participated in a successful joint attack on Fort Fisher near Wilmington, North Carolina, cutting off Robert E. Lee's supply lifeline to the Confederate capital of Richmond.

The Navy emerged from the Civil War larger, battle-hardened, and ready to return to its worldwide responsibilities. By 1867, more than half the ships in commission were serving overseas.

Steam, Steel, Empire, and Global War

In the years following the Civil War, the Navy began its usual peacetime decline in numbers and readiness but also experienced a technical and cultural revolution. Stephen Luce founded the Naval War College, and Alfred Thayer Mahan wrote his masterwork, *The Influence of Sea Power on History: 1660–1783*, which was to profoundly affect the course of naval thought for the next century. In 1885, the Navy's first true battleship, USS *Texas*, was commissioned and the United States would soon field a respectable battle-fleet as the then insular continental nation began to look outward.

In 1898, amid growing tension with Spain over Cuba, the USS *Maine* exploded and sank in Havana harbor under mysterious circumstances, sparking a war with Spain that left the United States victorious and in possession of a new overseas empire in the far Pacific. The Navy played a dominant role in the Spanish-American War, crushing Spanish fleets at Santiago de Cuba and Manila Bay in the Philippines, where Admiral Dewey famously uttered the phrase, "You may fire when ready, Gridley."

With this lopsided victory and President Theodore Roosevelt's encouragement, the U.S. Navy emerged as the symbol of a nation striding confidently onto the world stage. In 1907, Roosevelt launched the Great White Fleet on an around-the-world tour that underscored America's ascendancy. A few years earlier, in 1900, John Holland launched the first practical submarine, inaugurating a new chapter in naval warfare, and in 1910 Eugene Eli flew the first aircraft from a ship, taking off from USS *Birmingham*. In the years that followed, the Navy grew in size and competence, rivaling all but the British Royal Navy.

At the outbreak of the Great War in 1914, the United States attempted to stay out of yet another European conflict while the Navy prepared. Provoked by German unrestricted submarine warfare in the Atlantic, the United States finally declared war in 1917. In April 1917, U-boats sank more than 800,000 tons of allied shipping, pushing Britain to the brink of defeat. Help for the beleaguered British soon arrived in the form of a squadron of badly needed destroyers from the U.S. Navy. The British asked how soon the Americans could be ready for sea. CDR Joseph Taussig promptly replied, "We are ready now," and the Navy entered the desperate struggle to keep the Allied lifelines open in the Atlantic.

Following the "war to end all wars," the Navy's capabilities diminished rapidly, victim of isolationist sentiment, the Great Depression, and an international treaty limiting the size of all major navies. Despite this, the Navy continued its tradition of innovation in peacetime, experimenting with carrier aviation (the Navy's first aircraft carrier, USS *Langley*, was commissioned in 1920), replenishment at sea, and amphibious warfare. Submarines suitable for operating in the vast reaches of the Pacific Ocean were developed, radar made its appearance at sea, and antisubmarine sonar devices became a standard installation on escort vessels.

America's fighting role in World War II began with the Japanese aerial attack on Pearl Harbor on 7 December 1941. The Navy's battle fleet was destroyed, but the submarines were left untouched, and the four fleet aircraft carriers were at sea. Broadly, the war in the Pacific can be divided into three phases: A Japanese offensive that conquered the Philippines, Singapore, and much of the western Pacific; a period of stalemate as Japanese and U.S. forces slugged it out in the south Pacific, particularly in the Solomon Islands; and the epic drive across the central Pacific that ended in the defeat of Japan. While the Pacific war raged, the Navy also fought the grim struggle against the U-boats in the Atlantic and built up the armadas that would land vast armies in North Africa, Sicily, Italy, and, on 6 June 1944, the beaches of Normandy.

The Pacific war was a naval war fought on a scale and ferocity not seen before or since. The initial period of bitter defeats gave way in mid-1942 when the Japanese advance toward New Guinea and Australia was checked at the battle of Coral Sea, the first battle in history in which none of the opposing ships sighted each other. The aircraft carrier USS *Yorktown* suffered heavy bomb damage and limped back into Pearl Harbor to begin what was estimated to be three months of repairs. After less than three days of frantic work, she put to sea to join *Enterprise* and *Hornet*, then under the command of ADM Raymond Spruance, speeding toward Midway Island to meet the Japanese Combined Fleet. The "Miracle at Midway" was made up of equal parts luck, superb intelligence work, and traditional American aggressive initiative in battle. Four Japanese carriers were destroyed and their pilots killed while only the *Yorktown* was lost; the Japanese offensive was stopped forever.

Soon after Midway, the United States went on the offensive with a shoestring invasion of Guadalcanal where the Marines heroically earned a historic series of victories in the brutal island-hopping campaign across the Pacific. For months after the U.S. invasion, the fate of Guadalcanal was uncertain. The Navy suffered as it learned night fighting the hard way—the slot off Guadalcanal is a graveyard of so many ships that it became known as Iron Bottom Sound. When American fortunes were at their lowest ebb, a new commander, William "Bull" Halsey, was appointed, electrifying the Southwest Pacific Command. Halsey would go on to command the mighty Third Fleet, which led the drive on Japan, and retired as one of only four five-star admirals (the others are Chester Nimitz, the sure-handed Central Pacific Commander-in-Chief throughout the war; Ernie King, the CNO; and William Leahy, President Roosevelt's naval aide).

Eventually, the Americans overcame Japanese resistance and pushed on down the Solomon Islands chain. The seesaw fight in the Southwest Pacific closed with future CNO Arleigh Burke's "perfect battle" at Cape St. George, a night destroyer fight that went entirely the U.S. Navy's way. The Navy paid a dear price in the Solomon's campaign: After *Hornet* was sunk at the battle of Santa Cruz in October, the Americans in the Southwest Pacific were down to a single wounded carrier and one battleship. But within months the Navy offensive was on an unstoppable roll as American production poured ships and aircraft into the Pacific Theater even as the Allies landed in Italy and prepared for their storied surge across the English Channel. Also during this period the American submarine offensive, which began the day after the attack on Pearl Harbor with an order flashed across the Pacific to execute unrestricted submarine warfare against Japan, was beginning to inflict devastating loses on Japanese merchant shipping. Eventually Vice Admiral Lockwood's submarine force—which comprised less than 2 percent of active naval personnel—would strangle Japan's wartime economy, sinking 60 percent of all Japanese merchant shipping and 35 percent of her warship tonnage.

The great American drive across the Pacific steadily pushed back the Japanese defensive perimeter in 1944 and 1945 as one Japanese-occupied island after another fell. Titanic naval battles were fought at the Philippine Sea under ADM Raymond Spruance (a battle so one-sided it became known as "the Great Marianas Turkey Shoot" by VADM Marc Mitscher's naval aviators) and at Leyte Gulf. The battle of Leyte Gulf, which came

147

about because of a desperate attempt by the Japanese to throw back the American invasion of the Philippines, involved more ships and men than any other naval battle in history.

This battle featured the world's last battleship clash, when ADM Jesse Oldendorf's old battleships—raised from the mud of Pearl Harbor—crushed a Japanese force advancing through the dark of Surigao Strait, and the desperate fight of Taffy-3's tiny escort carriers and destroyers against Japanese battleships off Samar. Taffy-3's small force had been left exposed when Halsey's Task Force-38 lunged north, taking the bait of the last Japanese carriers deliberately dangled in front of him. Inexplicably, with the transports lying off the landing beaches practically under his guns, the Japanese commander turned back, unnerved by the ferocity of the American destroyer attacks. After Leyte, the Japanese Imperial Navy ceased to exist as an effective fighting force.

The last chapter of the Navy's war closed off the coast of Okinawa, a large Japanese home-island with a population of about a half million people. Spruance's fast carrier force struck relentlessly for 40 days and nights, supporting Marines ashore and protecting the landing beaches, within easy range of thousands of Japanese aircraft. More than 4,900 Sailors lost their lives holding the line at Okinawa, mostly victims of wave after wave of suicide attacks. Especially vulnerable were the gallant destroyers on radar picket duty on the fringes of the fleet. Many were sunk, and many more limped into port battered wrecks, barely afloat. The furious kamikaze onslaught at Okinawa was Japan's last spasm—a scant three months later USS *Missouri* led the way into Tokyo Bay to accept Japan's unconditional surrender. The Navy achieved its most lasting glory in the Pacific campaign, and this great drive across the Pacific occupies the very center of the U.S. Navy's cultural identity to this day.

Limited Wars and Cold Wars

World War II brought the world atomic bombs, missiles, and jet aircraft. Continuing the Navy's tradition of innovation in peacetime, some of the world's best engineers and leaders brought these advancements to the fleet: nuclear power, ballistic missiles, and the technical revolution that led to the familiar Aegis combat system at the heart of the modern surface combatant. Nuclear propulsion and jet aircraft were married in USS *Enterprise*, the first supercarrier.

Operationally, the Navy prepared to fight the Soviets at sea, most notably during the blockade of Cuba during the 1963 Cuban Missile Crisis, and in the 1980s Reagan-era buildup to the six-hundred-ship Navy led by Secretary of the Navy John Lehman, which was designed to challenge the

Soviets on their front doorstep. While preparing for blue water conflict at sea with the USSR, the Navy also participated in a series of limited wars and worked to prevent many more. Navy aircraft flew thousands of missions during the Korean and Vietnam wars. Among the heroic names that emerged from Vietnam, John McCain and VADM James Stockdale are representative of the hundreds of naval aviators shot down over North Vietnam who would return with honor after enduring years of brutality in North Vietnamese prison camps. Navy riverine squadrons fought on the Mekong Delta, reprising the brown water mission from the Civil War, and surface units spent weeks on gun-lines, providing fire-support to troops ashore. During later years of this conflict, CNO ADM Elmo Zumwalt initiated a series of long-overdue reforms to personnel and management policies that created the foundation for today's all-volunteer, highly professional Navy.

Carrier aircraft played vital roles in operations Desert Storm, Enduring Freedom, and Iraqi Freedom while the surface Navy added a new capability with precision strike Tomahawk land attack missiles. In a demonstration of the Navy's inherent flexibility and war-fighting readiness, warships arrived in the North Arabian Sea the day after the September 11, 2001, attacks. By 7 October, when the missile and air campaign against the Taliban began, more than fifty ships were on station. As the global war on terrorism continues today, Navy ships, submarines, and aircraft are patrolling around the world while tens of thousands of Sailors serve ashore in combat zones.

Through the long narrative of the U.S. Navy's history, certain threads run its entire length: aggressive initiative in battle, technical excellence and innovation, and forward-deployed presence around the world. The narrative continues today.

LCDR Jim Rushton is a surface warfare officer with more than twenty-five years of naval experience. A former limited duty officer and enlisted submariner, he has served sea tours in six warships and holds a master's degree in national security analysis from the Naval Postgraduate School.

Appendix 2
Useful Web Sites

For most of us who have earned a commission since the new millennium, the Internet has likely been our main source for information, communication, and entertainment. Our first instinct when confronted with an information need is to "Google" whatever topic we are looking for, but it is important to remember that online content is easily manipulated and sometimes flat out wrong. As you may remember from your academic experiences, the Internet is a tool to help you search and learn, but there is no substitute for conducting original research and thinking for yourself.

Of course, the Internet remains a valuable tool that will help you navigate your life at work and home. Listed below are categories with a few sites that are particularly relevant to a newly minted junior officer—particularly those with no prior military experience. As you browse these sites, you will find that their content will not necessarily reflect the opinions of the U.S. Navy. In fact, our inclusion of these sites does not constitute an endorsement of the products, services, or opinions you may encounter as you visit them, but this list represents the sites that many junior officers visit as they manage their lives in the Navy.

Career
★ Navy Personnel Command (www.npc.navy.mil)
★ BUPERS Online (https://www.bol.navy.mil)

The Navy Personnel Command (NPC) site has your detailer's contact information, slates, board information, community information, and much, much more. BUPERS Online contains all of your career information and qualifications in your officer data card as well as your fitness report history. NPC contains a lot of important information including critical information on promotion and screening boards, links to detailers, and any All Navy (ALNAV) or Naval Administration (NAVADMIN) message released since 2000.

Professional Development and Education
★ Navy Knowledge Online (www.nko.navy.mil)
★ Navy Professional Reading Program (www.navyreading.navy.mil)
★ Naval History & Heritage Command (www.history.navy.mil)

NKO is home for Navy e-learning, your electronic training jacket, career tools, online courses, and more. The Navy Professional Reading Program site, covered in more detail in appendix 3, contains several book collections along with a synopsis of each book. If you do not have an NKO account already, get one now. NKO is continually populated with tools for you and your Sailors, and you will be routinely required to complete NKO courses related to various programs and subjects that the Navy deems important. Finally, the Navy History & Heritage Command Web site is a terrific site to research naval history topics.

Family Readiness and Relocation

★ Ready.Gov (www.ready.gov)
★ Commander Navy Installations Command (https://www.cnic.navy.mil)
★ Smart Web Move (http://www.smartwebmove.navsup.navy.mil/)
★ Navy Exchange (NEX) Military Moving Center (https://www.military movingcenter.com/nexcom/)
★ Department of Defense Per Diem, Travel, and Transportation Allowances Committee (http://perdiem.hqda.pentagon.mil/perdiem/)
★ Great Schools (http://www.greatschools.net/)

Family readiness in the face of disaster is critical for Navy families who may be without their Sailor or in a new community. Ready.gov ensures that families are prepared for an emergency. The Commander Navy Installations Command site includes a number of links related to family readiness, including one to Operation Prepare, the Navy's site for family emergency readiness.

Relocation is also a way of life in the military. A number of Web sites can help reduce the time, stress, and confusion of permanent change of station (PCS) moves and temporary duty (TDY) travel. SmartWebMove, a NAVSUP Web site, allows members or their spouses to coordinate their household goods move through an online questionnaire. The NEX Military Moving Center is a portal to help you connect your utilities at your new place. The DoD per diem site is a clearinghouse for questions regarding per diem, basic allowance for housing (BAH), and travel or moves. Great Schools is an award-winning Web site that includes research, ratings, and testimonials for K–12 schools across the country.

Service-Related News and Entertainment

★ U.S. Navy official Web site (www.navy.mil)
★ U.S. Navy Public Affairs Resources (www.chinfo.navy.mil)
★ Military.com (www.military.com)

★ *Navy Times* (www.navytimes.com)
★ Get the Gouge (www.getthegouge.com)
★ Naval Institute Press (www.usni.org)
★ Information Dissemination (http://informationdissemination.blogspot.com)

To stay connected to the broader Navy, visit the Navy's official Web site regularly or the Navy's Chief of Information Site. Military.com has a wide variety of information and links for all members of the military, including pay and benefits, educational opportunities, military discounts, and current events. *Navy Times* is an unaffiliated Navy-specific Web site that is widely read for late-breaking news and commentary on important happenings. Get the Gouge is the U.S. Naval Institute's new, edgier, and entertaining portal for "the warrior" that complements its famous *Proceedings* magazine. The USNI is an independent forum that produces thoughtful periodicals, scholarly books, and stimulating conferences. Finally, the Information Dissemination blog provides some of the most in-depth and intellectually stimulating analysis on the net of where the U.S. Navy is headed. With their wealth of information and links, these sites are a great starting point for the latest and greatest in what is going on in the fleet—especially when you are "out of the loop" on deployment or on shore duty.

Community Sites and Blogs
★ SWONET (www.swonet.com)
★ Sailor Bob (www.sailorbob.com/phpBB2/index.php)
★ Naval Supply Systems Command (NAVSUP) homepage (https://www.navsup.navy.mil/navsup)
★ Air Warriors (http://www.airwarriors.com/)
★ CDR Salamander (http://cdrsalamander.blogspot.com/)
★ The Mudville Gazette (http://www.mudvillegazette.com/)
★ Warchop! (http://www.warchop.com)

Just as you see in the arenas of politics, business, and sports, most professionals seek out information from a combination of sources both official and informal, and naval officers are no exception. On the more officially managed side of Internet sites that you may find useful, SWONET is a surface warfare–centric site featuring bulletin boards of threaded discussions that registered members contribute to. NAVSUP has a direct link to the online version of the Supply Corps Newsletter, as well as NKO and the Naval Logistics Library (NLL).

In addition to the official sites, some blogs have both entertaining and informative posts that help the reader gain perspective and insights from members in their and other communities. Some sites, such as SailorBob and Warchop, are not officially affiliated with the military and serve as the electronic equivalent of talking with a large group of peers around the "water cooler." Just like real life water-cooler conversations, not everything you read on these sites may align with Navy policy and opinion, but it is foolish to ignore these sources of information and discussion just because they are not official sites.

Financial Sites
★ United Services Automobile Association (www.usaa.com)
★ Navy Federal Credit Union (www.navyfcu.org)
★ Mint.com (www.mint.com)
★ MyPay.com (https://mypay.dfas.mil/mypay.aspx)
★ Thrift Savings Plan (http://www.tsp.gov/index.html)

Although there are a wide array of financial service sites on the web, USAA and NFCU are two financial institutions that have enjoyed long-standing relationships with Navy personnel. Mint.com is an award-winning site that helps you track your spending and investments, breaks your spending down into easy-to-understand charts and graphs, and helps you budget your money. MyPay.com gives you access to your leave and earnings statements, W-2, and other pay-related links. The TSP site provides account access to participants' tax-deferred investment earnings and allocations.

Navy Family Support
★ Fleet and Family Support Center (https://www.nffsp.org/skins/nffsp/home.aspx)
★ U.S. Department of Defense Community Relations (www.americasupportsyou.mil)
★ MILSpouse.org (www.milspouse.org)
★ Military.com Discount Page (http://shock.military.com/DC/DealIndex.jsp)

The Military Family Network (http://www.emilitary.org/index.html)
There are a number of resources to help support Navy families. While the Fleet and Family Support Center's site is a great place to start, there are a number of sites that offer programs of support for Navy families. America Supports You is a DoD program that connects military members and their families to hundreds of organization dedicated to supporting our military

throughout the country. Additionally, there are a number of sites focused on providing military family members discounts or access to services. The discount page on Military.com allows users and merchants to list military specials. It also has a sort function that allows users to search for deals where they live. The Military Family Network site is a portal that links you to virtually all types of benefits, services, healthcare, employment opportunities, and more.

The Internet has changed our society, and the Navy is no exception. As with advice from your peers and more traditional media sources, you will be best served by seeking out information from a number of sources rather than relying solely on one source for all of your information. Nevertheless, the web is here to stay, and you should leverage that tool to the fullest in your journey as a newly commissioned officer.

Compiled and written by LT Micah Murphy and LT Rob Niemeyer.

Appendix 3
The Navy Professional Reading Program . . . and Beyond

What Is the Navy Professional Reading Program?

The Navy Professional Reading Program (NPRP) was designed and launched in 2006 to encourage service members to enhance their personal and professional development through a variety of popular and readily accessible books. The CNO, along with a cross section of military and academic professionals, carefully crafted five multiple book collections in an effort to "accelerate your mind." The books include traditional topics such as leadership, military heritage, and joint warfare, and then extend beyond military issues to incorporate cultural awareness, critical thinking, and management theory from the business world. The collections are geared toward various experience levels in the Navy, and there are terrific books on each list that you should certainly consider reading.

Why Should I Participate?

As a newly commissioned officer, your days (and nights) will likely feel more fully loaded than you have ever experienced. Job responsibilities, the pursuit of important warfare qualifications, family obligations, and a personal life are all things to balance. Among all these legitimate pursuits, however, reading is one that will replenish your mind with new ideas and new ways to look at the world. There is no requirement to delve into this program, but you may also be left on the sidelines of some great discussions among your coworkers if you opt to forgo reading as you progress in the Navy or in many other professions. There are many benefits to being a "lifelong learner." Reading can help you gain insight into:

★ The history of the naval service
★ Leadership principles from fictional and historical figures
★ Significant historical events
★ Behavioral and cultural differences
★ Parallels to the business world
★ Diverse perspectives on a variety of issues

If the above reasons are not enough, reading is also a proven way to relieve the stress of everyday life and work. It provides an escape from reality, even if just for a few minutes. If you are in an operational command, in particular, reading a few pages of a favorite book before turning in is one of the true small pleasures of life at sea.

How Does it Work?

The NPRP groups approximately sixty books into separate collections for five target audiences. The list for junior officers is titled "Division Leader Collection" and can be located at www.navyreading.navy.mil (or Google "Navy Professional Reading Program"). The other collections are titled "Junior Enlisted Collection," "Leading Petty Officer Collection," "Department/Command Leader Collection," and "Senior Leaders Collection."

Selected Readings for the Junior Officer

Borrowing heavily from the Navy Reading Web site's list and descriptions of the books that this superb Web site includes, below is a list of books for Junior Officers to consider. As you review this list, visit the Web site on your own to see if other books strike your interest.

Division Leader Collection
Management and Strategic Planning

Freakonomics: A Rogue Economist Explores the Hidden Side of Everything by Steven Levitt and Stephen Dubner

This 2005 *New York Times* best seller and cult favorite shows, through a mixture of amusing stories and copious data, that if the right questions are asked and the right incentives are unmasked, there is little behavior and few phenomena that cannot be explained. This book compels us to ask the right questions regarding how we create incentives to drive certain behaviors in the Navy, other organizations, and in greater society.

Innovator's Dilemma: The Revolutionary Book That Will Change the Way You Do Business by Clayton Christensen

Best-selling Harvard author Clayton Christensen warns us that even great organizations can falter if they fail to look ahead to "the next big thing,"—even if it initially meets opposition from others in the industry or the marketplace. Look for ways to apply what he calls "disruptive innovation" in your organization—your organization's future depends on it.

Leadership

Two Souls Indivisible: The Friendship That Saved Two POWs in Vietnam by James Hirsch

The story of how prisoners of war—an African American Air Force pilot and a white Navy pilot—overcame their differences in background and personality in a North Vietnamese POW camp, and how good people can survive by putting their differences aside and working together in the toughest environments imaginable. You can't pick who you work with and you won't always like all of your coworkers, but you will need to find a way to put differences and feelings aside to work together to accomplish the mission.

The Good Shepherd by C. S. Forester

Set during the beginning of World War II, Captain Krause is tasked with bringing a convoy of ships across the Atlantic as the German submarines attack the ships bound for England. Along the way, he is challenged to make difficult decisions, often with imperfect information, little time, and less-than-stellar equipment and personnel. Although this book contains the most realistic literary internal monologue of a commanding officer making decisions under stress, as a newly reported ensign you will undoubtedly see parallels between his and your situation—it is a primer for grace under pressure and success under duress.

Naval and Military Heritage

The Golden Thirteen: Recollections of the First Black Naval Officers edited by Paul Stillwell; foreword by Colin Powell

The stories of the first African American officers in the Navy and the background of how a group of prior enlisted Sailors transformed their own lives, the naval service, and society in general. No matter who you are or where you come from, you represent something bigger than yourself. What do you want your legacy to be? These inspirational stories will challenge you to answer that question.

Six Frigates: The Epic History of the Founding of the U.S. Navy by Ian Toll

This award-winning book details the original six frigates that created the foundation of the U.S. Navy in the years following the Revolutionary War. This book directly supports the efforts of the Master Chief Petty Officer of the Navy to "reinvigorate the fleet with a sense of our Navy's history and traditions" as published in *ALL HANDS*, June 2007.

Joint and Combined Warfare
Shield and Sword: The United States Navy in the Persian Gulf War edited by Edward Marolda and Robert Schneller Jr.

A historical account of the U.S. Navy's roles and perspective during the Persian Gulf War. This all-encompassing, maritime-focused book helps you understand what brought the United States to war in 1990–91 and the pivotal role that the Navy played in the war. This book highlights the successes and failures of operating in a joint atmosphere and underlines difficult leadership and command and control issues.

The Savage Wars of Peace: Small Wars and the Rise of American Power by Max Boot

This book summarizes the smaller-scale American wars and conflicts since the late 1700s, including their impact on U.S. foreign policy, and reminds the reader of their relevance to today's geopolitical climate. This book highlights the value of the U.S. Marine Corps' "Small Wars Manual" and shows leaders the importance of learning from our past and applying it to our future.

Regional and Cultural Awareness
On the Origins of War and the Preservation of Peace by Donald Kagan

Five case studies ranging from ancient to modern times that examine each nation's desire for peace and the decisions that led to war (or not, in the case of the Cuban missile crisis). This book emphasizes that decisions you make as a leader, no matter how small, have consequences. This book will teach you why we study history and will help you appreciate the tools of diplomacy and international relations.

Forgotten Continent: The Battle for Latin America's Soul by Michael Reid

Michael Reid, editor of *Economist*, investigates Latin America's expanding democracies and their growing impact in the world. This book's findings support the "Cooperative Strategy for the 21st Century" which "recognizes the rising importance and need for increased peacetime activities in Africa and the Western Hemisphere."

Critical Thinking
The World Is Flat: A Brief History of the 21st Century by Thomas Friedman

New York Times columnist Thomas Friedman explores the phenomenon of globalization in an easily understood and entertaining manner, particularly the telecommunications and technology advancements that have propelled globalization. As a country and as individuals, what are our opportunities and vulnerabilities in the future as the world continues to "flatten"?

Longitude: The True Story of a Lone Genius Who Solved the Greatest Scientific Problem of His Time by Dava Sobel

The true account of man's pursuit to solve one of the most compelling scientific quandaries of the 18th century—calculating longitude at sea. The story features John Harrison's race for a solution against better-known astronomers as life-changing prize money and prestige hang in the balance. You will never take a GPS for granted again after reading this critical-thinking masterpiece.

Noted Selections from Other Lists

A Sailor's History of the U.S. Navy by Thomas Cutler (Junior Enlisted Collection)

The 2006 Maritime Literature Award winner, now standard issue for every Sailor, is a "must read" for new officers, too. It gives a very readable, topically arranged account of the history of the sea service and important figures and events that shaped naval history. To adequately prepare for your future and that of the Navy, you must have a good grasp of its history . . . or you may be doomed to repeat it.

The Cruel Sea by Nicholas Monsarrat (Department/Command Leaders Collection)

One of the great novels of the sea, this tale of two World War II crews hunting German U-boats in the North Atlantic chronicles the transformation of a young recruit into a seasoned veteran, and a ship's captain into an ideal professional in command. Reading of the trials and challenges of this crew makes the modern reader ponder, how would I stack up in their situation?

Execution: The Discipline of Getting Things Done by Larry Bossidy and Ram Charan (Department/Command Leaders Collection)

This book could be retitled "The Art of Getting Things Done." The authors, a successful CEO and an executive advisor, guide the reader in the discipline of execution: understanding how to link together people, strategy, and operations, the three core elements of every business or organization. It's not enough to set the vision or dole out tasks, achieving success hinges upon the leaders' passionate engagement in all phases and facets of the mission.

The Crisis of Islam: Holy War and Unholy Terror by Bernard Lewis (Leading Petty Officers Collection)

To gain better insight into the mind of a radical Islamist and a greater cultural understanding of the forces shaping radical Islam, this concise, eye-opening book is a must-read in the post-9/11 world. To combat terrorism perpetrated by the practitioners of radical Islam, it is imperative to understand what fuels the rationale for their actions and sets their frame of reference.

Ender's Game by Orson Scott Card (Junior Enlisted Collection)

While it falls squarely within the science fiction genre, *Ender's Game* is really very much about a promising young military professional, training in strategy and tactics, honing his critical-thinking and leadership skills amid brutal training conditions. Think "*Harry Potter* meets *Band of Brothers*" . . . a pretty entertaining combination that results in one of the most readable and entertaining books on this list.

Starship Troopers by Robert Heinlein (Junior Enlisted Collection)

The 1959 winner of the Hugo Award, this science fiction classic describes the journey of young soldiers of the future as they endure the challenges of boot camp and the hardship of battle. Heinlein, a giant of science fiction and a former naval officer, wrote with a vividness and reality that will resonate for any serviceman in any era. This book stimulates thought about citizenship, responsibility, duty, and the role of the individual in society.

Where Do I Find These Books?

★ Your unit's library (each command has been given a full set)
★ Base library
★ Your local public library
★ The Navy Exchange (or www.navy-nex.com)—offers books up to 40 percent off the retail price
★ U.S. Naval Institute Press (www.usni.org)—offers discounts for members

Other ways to access these selections are to download them to your computer as "e-books" or listen to them as audio books.

To access books on NKO (https://www. nko.navy.mil), click on the "Reference" page. Then select "Econtent—Audio & eBooks" link on the left toolbar. Follow the instructions to download an e-book or an audio book. Within each application, you can search for books on the Navy Reading List and listen to or read them over your personal computer.

What Does the Future Hold for the Navy Reading Program?
Since its debut in fall 2006, the reading program has been extremely successful and continues to have strong commitment from the Chief of Naval Operations and the Master Chief Petty Officer of the Navy. While the book selection committee aims to pick "timeless" books for the collection, there are periodic reviews every eighteen to twenty-four months, so don't be surprised to see minor changes from time to time. Finally, keep your eye out for new technological avenues to deliver books to Sailors (other than e-books and audio books) to accommodate different learning styles.

Other Avenues to Accelerate Your Mind
The list above provides a wide range of superb books, but there are other reading sources available to broaden your mind.

Recommended Publications
The Economist. Published weekly, this magazine reports on worldwide events and topics that include politics, public policy, finance, and foreign relations. If you have time to read only one magazine a week, consider this one. If it is not your cup of tea, consider reading another weekly news magazine like *Time* or *Newsweek* for an efficient way to keep up with current events.

Foreign Affairs. Published quarterly (print and online at www.cfr.org), the Council of Foreign Relations nonpartisan information and analysis are great assets to understanding what is going on in the world around us and our potential role in shaping its future.

U.S. Naval Institute Proceedings. Published monthly by the U.S. Naval Institute, this publication is billed as "The Independent Forum on National Defense" and contains valuable insight, news, and advice for sea service professionals.

Harvard Business Review paperback series. Topics include leadership, high performance manager, managing projects, effective communication, and so on. www.hbsp.harvard.edu/hbsp/hbr/index.jsp

Recommended Podcasts
Leadership: Center for Creative Leadership (http://www.ccl.org/leadership/pod.xml)

Navy: CNO Podcast, Navy-Marine Corps Radio News (http://www.navy.mil/podcast/podcast.asp)

Leadership and Character in the Movies

Although movies focused on military leadership were most prevalent in the early post–World War II era, there are some more recent movies that explore the concepts of leadership and character. These films use both positive and negative examples and would be good candidates for individual viewing or for a professional movie night with your wardroom.

Military Leadership
We Were Soldiers
Saving Private Ryan
Master and Commander
Glory
Patton
The Great Escape
Gladiator
Gettysburg

Sports and Teamwork
Miracle
Remember the Titans
Rudy
Hoosiers

Organizational Behavior
12 Angry Men
Conspiracy
Glengarry Glen Ross

Compiled and written by LT Micah Murphy and LT Rob Niemeyer with deepest thanks to John Jackson, program manager of the Navy Reads Program, whose interview and written material, in addition to the Navy Reads Web site, provided the source material for the information included in this appendix.

Index

accountability, xv–xvi, 111

acronyms, vii–ix

admin office (ship's office), 14, 44–45, 46, 55, 57

administrative duties: "all but the signature" staffwork, 70–71; awards management, 76–78; classified material, 75, 78–80; counseling sheets, 75–76; discipline, 76; e-mail communications, 74–75; importance of, 70, 80; performance assessments, 75, 78; point paper, 73–74; reference library, 78; references, review of, 73; repetitive paperwork, 73; success in completing, 70–71; timeliness in completing, 71; writing style, 71–72

advancement. *See* promotions and career management

after-hours protocol, 23

Air Force Air Mobility Command (AMC) Space Available system, 48

alcohol and drug use, 67–68

allowances, 53

American Red Cross, 49–50

assessments and certifications, 112–13, 118–19

attitude, 119, 135–41

aviation career paths, 84

aviation engineering duty officers (EDO), 85–86

awards management, 76–78

Barbary Coast pirates, 143–44

Battle Efficiency Award, 77

bearing and character, 6, 40, 129–30, 140

benefits, 56–59

blogs, 153–54

Bluejacket's Manual (Cutler), 26–27

branch heads, 20

bunk and locker assignment, 17–18

Bureau of Naval Personnel (BUPERS): detailer, 81–82; education programs, 58, 91; On-Line (BOL) portal, 92, 151; orders, 12–13; promotion board, 81; screening board, 81; transfer/redesignation information, 93; Web site, 93, 151

burial at sea, 31

Burke, Arleigh, 19–20, 147

Care Line, 99

Career Compass (Winnefeld), 93

career paths. *See* promotions and career management

ceremonies and celebrations, 30–34, 96–97

certifications and assessments, 112–13, 118–19

chain of command, 20–21, 121–22

challenges and rewards, 11, 94, 102–4

change of command ceremonies, 30–31

chaplain corps, 88

character and bearing, 6, 40, 129–30, 140

charitable causes, 69

checklists (checksheets), 111–12, 116, 117

Chief of Naval Operations (CNO) Annual Guidance to the Navy, 62–63

chief petty officers (CPO), 23

chief warrant officers (CWO), 88, 90

165

About the Author

Fred W. Kacher is a 1990 graduate of the U.S. Naval Academy who has made multiple deployments at sea and has served on the staff of the Secretary of the Navy and in the White House. He currently serves as the first commanding officer of USS *Stockdale* (DDG 106). An author of numerous articles on naval leadership and management, this is his first book.

The **Naval Institute Press** is the book-publishing arm of the U.S. Naval Institute, a private, nonprofit, membership society for sea service professionals and others who share an interest in naval and maritime affairs. Established in 1873 at the U.S. Naval Academy in Annapolis, Maryland, where its offices remain today, the Naval Institute has members worldwide.

Members of the Naval Institute support the education programs of the society and receive the influential monthly magazine *Proceedings* or the colorful bimonthly magazine *Naval History* and discounts on fine nautical prints and on ship and aircraft photos. They also have access to the transcripts of the Institute's Oral History Program and get discounted admission to any of the Institute-sponsored seminars offered around the country.

The Naval Institute's book-publishing program, begun in 1898 with basic guides to naval practices, has broadened its scope to include books of more general interest. Now the Naval Institute Press publishes about seventy titles each year, ranging from how-to books on boating and navigation to battle histories, biographies, ship and aircraft guides, and novels. Institute members receive significant discounts on the Press's more than eight hundred books in print.

Full-time students are eligible for special half-price membership rates. Life memberships are also available.

For a free catalog describing Naval Institute Press books currently available, and for further information about joining the U.S. Naval Institute, please write to:

Member Services
U.S. Naval Institute
291 Wood Road
Annapolis, MD 21402-5034
Telephone: (800) 233-8764
Fax: (410) 571-1703
Web address: www.usni.org